Bridging the Gap

Strategies for Connecting with Patients' Families in Healthcare

Clear and compassionate communication can transform patient care. "Bridging the Gap" provides doctors with essential strategies to connect with patients and their families.

Learn how to manage difficult conversations, provide reassurance, and deliver complex information with clarity and empathy. This book is a cornerstone for any medical professional seeking to enhance their communication skills.

Author :

Dr.Raghavendra Prasad
MBBS,DA,FIPM.

---- *As patients recover, relatives' doubts and bitterness dissolve into gratitude. Successful outcomes highlight the dedication of healthcare professionals, fostering trust and admiration. Healing strengthens the bond between medical staff and families, marking a journey from skepticism to appreciation*

---- *Effective communication, counseling, and emotional support for patient relatives are vital for doctors, patients, and the entire medical system. They not only promote understanding, trust, and cooperation but also enable doctors to maintain peak efficiency in their work, leading to better outcomes for patients and overall healthcare delivery.*

My father is the best person in my life. He played with us, listened to our stories, fulfilled all our desires, and stood by us during bad times. He struggled all his life to make us happy and strong, never letting us realize the extent of his hardships. He helped anyone who crossed his path, even those who had wronged him, forgiving them without hesitation.

Every day, I strive to be like you.

Contents

Foreword

In the high-pressure world of healthcare, effective communication is often the cornerstone of patient care and satisfaction. Every day, doctors and healthcare professionals navigate the delicate balance between providing top-notch medical care and addressing the concerns and emotions of patients' families. This book, "Bridging the Gap: Strategies for Connecting with Patients' Families in Healthcare," is a timely and essential guide for every medical professional committed to excellence in their practice.

The need for such a book has never been greater. In an era where medical advancements are rapid and patient expectations are high, the ability to communicate clearly, compassionately, and effectively can make a profound difference in the healthcare experience. Poor communication can lead to misunderstandings, increased stress, and even conflict, whereas strong, empathetic communication can build trust, alleviate anxiety, and foster a cooperative environment.

"Bridging the Gap" offers a to-the-point approach, presenting practical strategies and real-world s to help doctors and healthcare professionals handle the most challenging interactions with patients' families. Drawing on proven communication techniques, this book provides tools to manage crises, navigate emotionally charged dialogues, and resolve conflicts with grace and confidence.

As a healthcare professional, you will find the insights and strategies within these pages invaluable for maintaining your efficiency and effectiveness, even in the most stressful conditions. For readers and fellow doctors embarking on this journey of enhanced communication, I extend my best wishes. May this book serve as a beacon, guiding you to build stronger, more trusting relationships with your patients and their families, ultimately leading to improved patient outcomes and a more harmonious healthcare environment. Here's to bridging the gap and fostering a more compassionate and communicative future in healthcare.

Warm regards,

Dr. Satyajit Kumar Singh

Urology & Andrology/Managing Director,Ruban Memorial Hospital,Patliputra,Patna

Introduction

In the complex and often emotionally charged environment of healthcare, effective communication is paramount. Nowhere is this more evident than in interactions between medical professionals and patients' relatives. These interactions can be fraught with challenges, ranging from misunderstandings and frustrations to outright hostility. However, by employing proven communication strategies, healthcare providers can navigate these challenges and foster constructive dialogue that promotes understanding and collaboration.

In this book, we delve into the intricacies of effective communication and counseling when dealing with patients' relatives. Drawing from real-life s and utilizing strategies outlined in "Crucial Conversations: Tools for Talking When Stakes Are High" by Kerry Patterson, Joseph Grenny, Ron McMillan, and Al Switzler, we explore how healthcare professionals can address common concerns and conflicts while maintaining professionalism and empathy.

Understanding Patients' Relatives Concerns

We begin by examining the diverse concerns that patients' relatives may express during their interactions with healthcare providers. From dissatisfaction with diagnosis and treatment to issues with communication and staff behavior, these concerns often stem from fear, uncertainty, and a desire for the best possible care for their loved ones. Each concern presents a unique challenge for healthcare providers, requiring tailored approaches to address effectively.

Navigating Common Communication Traps

In the midst of emotional and high-stakes conversations, it's easy to fall into common communication traps that can hinder productive dialogue. We explore these traps, such as silence, violence, assumptions, and biased stories, and discuss strategies for avoiding them. By recognizing and sidestepping these pitfalls, healthcare providers can maintain open lines of communication and foster trust with patients' relatives.

Choosing Effective Communication Strategies

Effective communication is not one-size-fits-all. It requires adaptability and a willingness to tailor approaches to the specific situation and individuals involved. We delve into a range of communication strategies, from asking for others' paths and making it safe to mastering our stories and stating our perspectives confidently. By choosing the best strategy for each interaction, healthcare providers can navigate crucial conversations successfully and build stronger connections with patients' relatives.

Conclusion

In the pages that follow, we explore real-life s, employing the strategies outlined above to address concerns and conflicts in healthcare settings. Through these examples, we aim to equip healthcare providers with the tools and insights needed to communicate effectively and compassionately with patients' relatives, ultimately enhancing the quality of care and fostering positive outcomes for all involved.

Gratitude Letter to the Authors of "Crucial Conversations: Tools for Talking When Stakes Are High"

Dear Kerry Patterson, Joseph Grenny, Ron McMillan, and Al Switzler,

I am writing to extend my heartfelt gratitude to you for your exceptional work in "Crucial Conversations: Tools for Talking When Stakes Are High." Your insightful ideas and strategies have served as a beacon of inspiration for me in my journey to enhance communication in healthcare settings.

Your book has not only provided valuable insights into effective communication but has also equipped me with practical tools to navigate crucial conversations with patients and their families. Drawing from your wisdom, I have incorporated these strategies into my own book, titled "Bridging the Gap: Strategies for Connecting with Patients' Families in Healthcare."

Your profound guidance has not only enriched my understanding but has also enabled me to foster stronger connections with patients and their families. By applying the principles outlined in your book, I aim to create a more supportive and empathetic environment within healthcare facilities.

Once again, I express my deepest appreciation for your invaluable contribution to the field of communication. Your work continues to inspire and guide healthcare professionals like myself in delivering compassionate care to those in need.

Concept of Skill as discussed "Crucial Conversations: Tools for Talking When Stakes Are High" by Kerry Patterson (Author), Joseph Grenny (Author), Ron McMillan (Author), Al Switzler (Author)

Avoiding Obvious Traps:
Skillful communicators recognize and sidestep common pitfalls that hinder productive dialogue.
These traps can sabotage effective communication.
Here are some examples:
Silence or Violence:
Silence: Occurs when we withhold our thoughts, feelings, or concerns. It's like bottling up emotions, which can lead to resentment or misunderstanding.
Violence: Manifests as aggressive behavior, verbal attacks, or shouting. It escalates conflicts and damages relationships.
Labeling and Stereotyping:
Instead of labeling people (e.g., "lazy," "stubborn") or making assumptions based on stereotypes, skillful communicators focus on understanding individual perspectives.

Avoiding the Issue:
Some people divert from the main topic by discussing irrelevant matters. Skillful communicators stay on track and address the core issue.

Winning at All Costs:
The desire to win an argument can lead to destructive communication. Skillful communicators prioritize understanding, resolution, and maintaining relationships over winning.

Making Assumptions:
Skillful communicators seek clarity rather than assuming intentions or motives. They ask questions to understand better.

Mind Reading:
Avoid assuming you know what others are thinking. Instead, ask open-ended questions to explore their perspective.

Righteousness:
Being right isn't always the goal. Skillful communicators focus on finding common ground and mutual understanding.

Avoiding the Fool's Choice:
The fool's choice is the false belief that we must choose between telling the truth and maintaining relationships. Skillful communicators find ways to do both.

Biased Stories:
Skillful communicators separate facts from their interpretations or stories. They recognize that their stories may not be accurate.

The Sucker's Choice: This trap involves believing we must choose between two undesirable options. Skillful communicators explore creative solutions to avoid this false dilemma.

False Dilemmas: Avoid presenting situations as black-and-white choices. Skillful communicators consider multiple perspectives.

The Blame Game: Instead of blaming others, skillful communicators focus on shared responsibility and collaborative solutions.

Choosing the Best Strategy: Skillful communicators adapt their approach based on the situation. Effective strategies include:

Ask for Others' Paths: Understand their viewpoints, intentions, and feelings. Encourage open dialogue.

Make It Safe: Create a safe environment for discussion. Safety encourages honesty and openness.

Master My Stories: Recognize and challenge unhelpful narratives. Our interpretations shape our reality, so skillful communicators examine their stories.

STATE My Path: Share your perspective confidently, humbly, and skillfully. Use "STATE" as an acronym: Share your facts, Tell your story, Ask for others' paths, Talk tentatively, and Encourage testing. Remember, skillful communication is an ongoing process. By avoiding traps and choosing effective strategies, we can navigate crucial conversations successfully and build stronger connections.

Examples of concerns and issues with relatives

1. First Encounter at emergency department.
2. Who is the doctor you or me.
3. Appropriate diagnosis is not being made.
4. Irrelevant investigations are being ordered.
5. Too much and costly medicines are being used.
6. Patient is not improving, ICU stay is prolonged.
7. Appropriate communication with relatives is not being made.
8. They are not allowed to see their patients frequently.
9. Patient is not getting adequate food and water.
10. Diaper change is not done on time.
11. Doctor is giving false hope about the patient.
12. Patient was better but doctor's interventions have made the patient worse,
13. Inappropriate billing is being done.
14. Behavior of hospital staff, guard, nurse, and ward boys are very rude.
15. Patient is dead but he is forcefully kept on ventilator and life support.
16. No one is listening when we are calling for the nurse.
17. Paperwork takes too much of time.
18. Few relatives are inherently ill-mouthed and rude.
19. Change my doctor I am not satisfied.
20. My patient came walking and he was all well before.
21. Change in diagnosis and specialist.

22. When nothing is working - end of life.

23. Breaking the bad news,

24. Patient is alive but you are calling him dead,

25. Explaining for organ donation.

To effectively address the concerns of patient relatives and manage communication in critical situations, we can outline a comprehensive plan that incorporates strategies from "Crucial Conversations" and covers key aspects such as emotional support, anxiety, concerns, fear, expenses, stay, level of care, avoiding errors, timely diagnosis, and appropriate investigations and treatment.

Key Points to Cover in Communication with Patient Relatives:

1. Emotional Support:
- Acknowledge their feelings and provide empathy.
- Reassure them that the medical team is doing everything possible.

2. Managing Anxiety and Concerns:
- Provide clear and regular updates on the patient's status.
- Offer realistic expectations about potential outcomes.

3. Addressing Fear:
- Explain the procedures, treatments, and their purposes.
- Be transparent about the risks and benefits.

4. Discussing Expenses:
- Provide a clear breakdown of costs and available financial assistance.
- Discuss insurance coverage and payment plans if needed.

5. Stay and Level of Care:
- Inform them about the expected duration of stay.
- Assure them about the quality of care and the qualifications of the medical team.

6. Avoiding Errors:

- Explain the measures in place to prevent medical errors.
- Encourage them to speak up if they notice something amiss.

7. Timely and Accurate Diagnosis:
- Discuss the diagnostic process and how it guides treatment.
- Inform them about the expected time frame for results.

8. Appropriate Investigations and Treatment:
- Justify the necessity of each investigation and treatment.
- Address any concerns about the relevance and cost of procedures.

Strategies for Crucial Conversations:

1. Start with Heart:
- Begin the conversation with genuine concern for the patient's well-being.
- Focus on the common goal of the patient's recovery.

2. Learn to Look:
- Be attentive to verbal and non-verbal cues from relatives.
- Address any signs of distress or confusion immediately.

3. Make It Safe:
- Create a safe environment for open dialogue.
- Ensure that relatives feel comfortable expressing their concerns.

4. Master My Stories:
- Stick to the facts and avoid assumptions or interpretations.
- Share your perspective calmly and listen actively to theirs.

5. State My Path:
- Clearly articulate your point of view and the reasoning behind decisions.
- Use "I" statements to avoid sounding accusatory or defensive.

6. Explore Others' Paths:

- Invite relatives to share their thoughts and feelings.

- Validate their concerns and acknowledge their perspective.

7. Move to Action:

- Collaboratively decide on the next steps.

- Ensure there is a clear plan moving forward and that everyone understands it.

Plan and Principles for Major Concerns and Issues with Relatives:

1. First Encounter at Emergency Department:
- Greet relatives warmly and introduce yourself.
- Provide a brief update on the patient's condition and the immediate steps being taken.

2. Who is the Doctor You or Me:
- Clarify the roles and responsibilities of the medical team.
- Reassure them of the collaborative approach to patient care.

3. Appropriate Diagnosis is Not Being Made:
- Explain the diagnostic process and the time it takes.
- Discuss the rationale behind current and future tests.

4. Irrelevant Investigations are Being Ordered:
- Justify the necessity of each test and its relevance to the patient's condition.
- Address any concerns about cost and invasiveness.

5. Too Much and Costly Medicines are Being Used:
- Provide a rationale for each prescribed medication.
- Discuss cost-effective alternatives if available.

6. Patient is Not Improving, ICU Stay is Prolonged:
- Give regular updates on the patient's progress.

- Discuss the challenges and the steps being taken to address them.

7. Appropriate Communication with Relatives is Not Being Made:
- Establish regular communication channels.
- Schedule updates and be available for questions.

8. They are Not Allowed to See Their Patients Frequently:
- Explain visitation policies and their reasons.
- Make exceptions or offer virtual visits if possible.

9. Patient is Not Getting Adequate Food and Water:
- Reassure them of the patient's nutritional and hydration management.
- Address any specific dietary concerns.

10. Diaper Change is Not Done on Time:
- Ensure proper hygiene practices are followed.
- Address specific instances and reassure them of care standards.

11. Doctor is Giving False Hope about the Patient:
- Provide honest and realistic updates.
- Discuss potential outcomes candidly.

12. Patient was Better but Doctor's Interventions have Made the Patient Worse:

- Explain the necessity of interventions and potential risks.
- Discuss the steps being taken to address complications.

13. Inappropriate Billing is Being Done:
    - Provide a detailed billing statement.
    - Address any discrepancies and offer clarification.

14. Behavior of Hospital Staff, Guard, Nurse, and Ward Boys are Very Rude:
    - Listen to their complaints and take them seriously.
    - Assure them that corrective measures will be taken.

15. Patient is Dead but He is Forcefully Kept on Ventilator and Life Support:
    - Explain the medical criteria for continuing life support.
    - Discuss end-of-life care options sensitively.

16. No One is Listening When We are Calling for the Nurse:
    - Ensure that the nursing staff is responsive.
    - Address specific instances and improve response protocols.

17. Paperwork Takes Too Much Time:
    - Streamline paperwork processes.
    - Provide assistance in filling out necessary forms.

18. Few Relatives are Inherently Ill-Mouthed and Rude:
    - Handle difficult relatives with patience and empathy.

- Set boundaries while maintaining professionalism.

19. Change My Doctor I am Not Satisfied:
    - Discuss their concerns and offer to arrange for a different doctor if needed.
    - Reassure them of continuous and consistent care.

20. My Patient Came Walking and He Was All Well Before:
    - Explain the progression of the illness or condition.
    - Discuss the treatment plan and expected outcomes.

21. Change in Diagnosis and Specialist:
    - Justify the current diagnosis and treatment plan.
    - Offer a second opinion if necessary.

22. When Nothing is Working End of Life:
    - Discuss palliative care and end-of-life options.
    - Provide emotional support and address their concerns sensitively.

23. Breaking the Bad News:
    - Use a compassionate and clear approach.
    - Provide space for them to process the information and ask questions.

24. Patient is Alive but You are Calling Him Dead:
    - Clarify the medical condition and criteria for declaring death.
    - Offer additional explanations and support.

25. Persuasion for Organ Donation:
   - Approach the topic sensitively and provide all necessary information.
   - Respect their decision and offer support regardless of the outcome.
   By addressing these points and following the principles of effective communication, we can ensure that relatives feel informed, supported, and involved in the patient's care, ultimately improving the overall experience during difficult times.

1.First encounter at the emergency department. Communication with Anxious Relatives in the Emergency Department

Setting: Emergency Department, Hospital

Characters:
- Dr. Brown: Resident doctor in the emergency department.
- Mr. and Mrs. Singh: Relatives of the patient.
- Patient: Mr. Singh's father, admitted with severe symptoms.

Narrator:
Mr. Singh's father has been brought to the emergency department with severe symptoms. Dr. Brown must explain the need for ICU admission and the process of diagnosis and treatment to the anxious relatives.

Dr. Brown (calmly and reassuringly):
"Mr. and Mrs. Singh, thank you for coming. I understand that this is a very stressful time for you. Your father's condition is serious, and we need to admit him to the ICU for closer monitoring and intensive care."

Mr. Singh (anxiously):

"But why can't a specialist see him right now? Why are we waiting for tests? We need to know exactly what's wrong with him!"

Mrs. Singh (tearfully):
"We just want to make sure he's getting the best care. Why can't you tell us everything now?"

Dr. Brown (making it safe and sharing facts):
"I completely understand your concern. Right now, our priority is to stabilize him and make sure he is as comfortable as possible. We have already started running some basic tests to understand the severity of his condition. These tests will give us important information that will help us make an accurate diagnosis."

Mr. Singh (still worried):
"But what if it's something very serious? Shouldn't a specialist be here right away?" Dr. Brown (talking tentatively and making it safe):
"It's natural to want immediate answers, especially when someone you love is in pain. The specialists are indeed available and will be consulted as soon as we have the initial test results. This way, they can provide the most informed and effective treatment plan based on accurate information."

Mrs. Singh (calming slightly):
"So, what happens now? What should we expect?"

Dr. Brown (sharing the plan and providing reassurance):
"Right now, we are admitting him to the ICU where he will be closely monitored by our skilled team. We will start treatment based on his current symptoms and the provisional diagnosis we can make from initial observations. Once we have the results from these basic tests, we will consult with the relevant specialists to get a comprehensive diagnosis and treatment plan."

Mr. Singh (more composed):
"How long will this take? When will we know more?"

Dr. Brown (setting expectations and building trust):
"The initial tests should be back within a few hours. During this time, our team will ensure he is stable and comfortable. Once we have the results, we will immediately bring in the specialists to evaluate him further. I promise to keep you informed every step of the way and answer any questions you may have."

Mrs. Singh (nodding):
"Thank you, Doctor. We just want to make sure we're doing everything we can for him."

Dr. Brown (compassionately):
"I understand completely. We are committed to providing the best care possible and making sure he gets the right diagnosis and treatment. Please, if you have any concerns or need more information, don't

hesitate to ask. We're here to support you and your family through this."

Mr. Singh (relieved):
"Thank you, Dr. Brown. We appreciate your help and understanding."

Dr. Brown (smiling reassuringly):
"You're welcome. We'll take good care of him and keep you updated. Let's focus on getting him the care he needs right now."

Narrator:
Through calm, empathetic communication, Dr. Brown was able to reassure Mr. and Mrs. Singh about the process of diagnosis and treatment. By sharing facts, making it safe for them to express their concerns, and providing clear information about what to expect, Dr. Brown helped alleviate their anxiety and built trust in the medical team.

Analysis of Communication Strategies Utilized

1. Empathy and Compassion:
- What Dr. Brown did: Acknowledged the relatives' stress and emotional pain.
- Purpose: Builds trust and rapport, making it easier for the relatives to process difficult information.

Example:
> "I understand that this is a very stressful time for you. Your father's condition is serious, and we need to admit him to the ICU for closer monitoring and intensive care."

2. Sharing Facts and Telling the Story:
- What Dr. Brown did: Explained the current situation and the necessity of tests for accurate diagnosis.
- Purpose: Provides clarity and helps the relatives understand the process.

Example:
> "We have already started running some basic tests to understand the severity of his condition.
These tests will give us important information that will help us make an accurate diagnosis."

3. Making It Safe and Talking Tentatively:
- What Dr. Brown did: Used gentle language and acknowledged the relatives' need for immediate answers.
- Purpose: Reduces defensive reactions and makes it easier for the relatives to express their concerns.

Example:

> "It's natural to want immediate answers, especially when someone you love is in pain."

4. Setting Expectations and Building Trust:

- What Dr. Brown did: Provided a timeline for test results and next steps.
- Purpose: Helps the relatives feel informed and reassured about the care process.

Example:

> "The initial tests should be back within a few hours. During this time, our team will ensure he is stable and comfortable."

5. Offering Additional Support:

- What Dr. Brown did: Encouraged the relatives to ask questions and expressed a commitment to keeping them informed.
- Purpose: Provides a sense of security and ensures the relatives know they are not alone.

Example:

> "Please, if you have any concerns or need more information, don't hesitate to ask. We're here to support you and your family through this."

2.Who is the Doctor you or me - Initial Conversation and Tension

Setting: Emergency Department

Characters:
Dr. Smith: The doctor on duty.
Mr. and Mrs. Johnson: Relatives of the patient.
Patient: In a bed nearby, experiencing abdominal pain.

Narrator:
The patient has been brought to the emergency department with severe abdominal pain. Dr. Smith has conducted initial tests and diagnosed a myocardial infarction. The doctor approaches Mr. and Mrs. Johnson to explain the diagnosis.

Dr. Smith (calmly at first):
"Mr. and Mrs. Johnson, I've reviewed the tests and it appears that your loved one is having a heart attack. While the pain is in the abdomen, this can sometimes be a sign of a heart issue due to referred pain."

Mr. Johnson (confused and skeptical):
"A heart attack? But he's only been complaining about his stomach. How can that be related to his heart?"

Mrs. Johnson (worried):

"This doesn't make sense. He didn't have any chest pain. Are you sure it's not something else, like a stomach problem?"

Dr. Smith (becoming frustrated):
"I understand this can be confusing, but the tests are very clear. This is a myocardial infarction. Abdominal pain can be a symptom of this."

Mr. Johnson (raising his voice):
"No, we know him. It's just a stomach issue. Are you sure you're not missing something?"

Dr. Smith (losing patience and shouting):
"Who is the doctor here, you or me? Let me do my job and diagnose the patient. This is a heart attack, and we need to act quickly!"

Narrator:
Stunned by the doctor's aggressive response, Mr. and Mrs. Johnson fall silent. However, the abruptness and disrespect of the doctor's outburst leave them feeling hurt and mistrustful. They quietly discuss their doubts and frustrations among themselves.

Mrs. Johnson (whispering to Mr. Johnson):
"I don't trust him. How can he be so sure when it's just stomach pain?"

Mr. Johnson (nodding):

"We'll have to watch closely. I don't like how he handled this."

Narrator:
As Dr. Smith walks away to arrange further treatment, he feels a mix of frustration and concern. The relatives' lack of understanding and trust weighs heavily on him, creating a tense and unproductive atmosphere.

Analysis

Relatives' Perspective:
 Confusion and Concern: The relatives are genuinely confused about the diagnosis and concerned about the patient.
 Feeling Disrespected: The doctor's aggressive response makes them feel unheard and disrespected.
 Mistrust: The initial communication mishandles their concerns, leading to a buildup of mistrust and a grudge against the doctor.

Doctor's Perspective:
 Frustration: Dr. Smith is under pressure to provide urgent care and feels frustrated that the relatives are not accepting the serious diagnosis.
 Miscommunication: The doctor's aggressive response further alienates the relatives, making it harder to provide effective care.

Transition to Improved Communication

Narrator:
Realizing the damage caused by the initial
confrontation, Dr. Smith takes a moment to reflect and
decides to rebuild trust and effectively communicate
the seriousness of the situation.

Dr. Smith (calmly and empathetically):
"Mr. and Mrs. Johnson, I apologize for raising my voice
earlier. I understand how stressful and confusing this
must be for you. Let's sit down and go over the test
results together so you can understand why we believe
this is a heart attack."

Mr. Johnson (still cautious):
"Okay, we just want to make sure we understand
what's happening."

Mrs. Johnson (nodding):
"Yes, please explain it to us."

Dr. Smith (sharing facts and telling the story):
"Of course. Here's what we found..."

By taking this step, Dr. Smith aims to rebuild trust and
provide the relatives with the clarity and support they

need, demonstrating a more effective approach to crucial conversations.

Rebuilding Trust

Dr. Smith (calmly and empathetically):
"I apologize if my previous response was harsh. I understand this is a very stressful situation for you both. Let's talk through this so you can understand what's happening."

Mr. Johnson (concerned):
"We just don't understand how abdominal pain can mean a heart attack."

Dr. Smith (Sharing facts):
"It's a great question. Sometimes, the pain from a heart attack can be felt in different parts of the body, including the abdomen. It's what we call referred pain."

Mrs. Johnson:
"But we've never heard of this before."

Dr. Smith (Telling the story):
"I know it's not commonly known, but the heart and abdomen are connected through the nervous system. When the heart is in distress, the pain signals can be felt in the abdomen. The tests we've run, including the EKG and blood tests, strongly indicate a heart attack."

Mr. Johnson (still skeptical):
"It's hard to believe."

Dr. Smith (Making it safe):
"I understand. Your concerns are completely valid. It's important to me that you feel comfortable and informed about the diagnosis. Do you have any specific questions or concerns about the tests or the diagnosis?"

Mrs. Johnson:
"We're just scared and confused."

Dr. Smith (Talking tentatively and encouraging testing):
"I can only imagine how difficult this must be. What we're seeing in the tests is very clear, but I want to ensure you have all the information you need. We can go through the test results together, and I'm also open to arranging a second opinion if that would help you feel more confident in the diagnosis."

Mr. Johnson:
"Thank you. We'd like to understand the test results better."

Dr. Smith (Creating a collaborative environment):
"Absolutely. Let's sit down and review them together. And please, feel free to ask any questions you have as we go through this."

Mrs. Johnson:
"Okay, that sounds good. We just want to be sure."

Dr. Smith:
"I appreciate that. Your involvement is crucial in ensuring the best care for your loved one. Let's start with the EKG results..."

Reviewing Test Results and Building Understanding

Dr. Smith leads Mr. and Mrs. Johnson to a nearby consultation area where they can sit comfortably.

Dr. Smith:
"Here are the EKG results. The EKG measures the electrical activity of the heart. These particular patterns we're seeing indicate that there's been damage to the heart muscle, which is consistent with a heart attack."

Mr. Johnson:
"Can you show us exactly what you mean?"

Dr. Smith (pointing to the EKG printout):
"Of course. See these elevated segments here? This elevation, along with the patient's symptoms and other test results, is what we typically see in a heart attack. Additionally, the blood tests showed elevated levels of

cardiac enzymes, which are released when the heart muscle is damaged."

Mrs. Johnson:
"So, the pain he felt in his stomach was actually coming from his heart?"

Dr. Smith:
"Yes, that's correct. It's not uncommon for heart attack symptoms to be felt in the abdomen, back, neck, or jaw. It's why heart attacks can sometimes be mistaken for other conditions."

Mr. Johnson:
"I see. But why did you get so upset earlier?"

Dr. Smith (apologetically):
"I'm truly sorry about that. The urgency of the situation can sometimes lead to stress, and my frustration was not directed at you personally. I want to ensure we're all on the same page for the best possible outcome for your loved one."

Mrs. Johnson: "We appreciate your explanation. What happens next?"

Dr. Smith:
"The next steps are crucial. We need to administer medications to help dissolve any clots and possibly prepare for a procedure to restore blood flow to the

heart. Time is of the essence in these situations to minimize damage to the heart."

Mr. Johnson:
"What kind of procedure are we talking about?"

Dr. Smith:
"If needed, we might perform an angioplasty, where we insert a small balloon to open up the blocked artery, or place a stent to keep it open. I'll walk you through everything step by step, and we'll monitor his progress closely."

Mrs. Johnson:
"And you're sure this is the best course of action?"

Dr. Smith (confidently but humbly):
"Yes, based on the tests and his current condition, this is the best approach. But I also respect your need for reassurance. If you want, we can consult with another cardiologist to confirm the treatment plan."

Mr. Johnson: "No, I think we understand better now. Thank you for taking the time to explain everything."

Dr. Smith:
"You're welcome. I'm here to answer any more questions you have and to support you through this process. Let's focus on getting the best care for your loved one."

Conclusion

By using the strategies Dr. Smith shifts from an aggressive, defensive stance to a collaborative, informative approach. This helps build trust, alleviate the relatives' concerns, and ensures they feel involved and respected in the decisionmaking process. The doctor's willingness to explain, listen, and offer options for additional reassurance creates a safer and more supportive environment for the

3.Appropriate diagnosis is not being made

The emergency room was bustling with activity as Dr. Smith hurried from one patient to another. Suddenly, a commotion caught his attention. A distressed woman was berating one of the nurses at the reception desk. Dr. Smith recognized her as Mrs. Johnson, whose husband had been admitted earlier that day with mysterious symptoms.

Approaching Mrs. Johnson, Dr. Smith greeted her calmly, "Mrs. Johnson, is everything alright? How can I assist you today?"

Mrs. Johnson's eyes flashed with frustration as she launched into her tirade, "Dr. Smith, we've been here for hours, and nobody seems to know what's wrong with my husband! Your tests are useless, and your staff is incompetent!"

Dr. Smith took a deep breath, reminding himself to avoid obvious traps in the conversation. He knew that reacting defensively or engaging in a shouting match would only escalate the situation. Instead, he chose to maintain a composed demeanor and focus on understanding Mrs. Johnson's concerns.

"I understand that this must be incredibly frustrating for you, Mrs. Johnson," Dr. Smith began empathetically. "We're doing everything we can to determine the cause of your husband's symptoms, but sometimes, diagnosis can be challenging, especially with complex cases like his." Mrs. Johnson's shoulders tensed, but Dr. Smith continued, "Can you tell me more about how your husband has been feeling? Any changes in his symptoms since we last spoke?"

As Mrs. Johnson recounted her husband's symptoms, Dr. Smith listened attentively, making sure to avoid making assumptions or labeling their situation. He focused on gathering as much information as possible to help guide the next steps in his patient's care.

Once Mrs. Johnson finished speaking, Dr. Smith took a moment to summarize what he had heard. "Thank you for sharing that with me, Mrs. Johnson. Based on what you've described, I think it's essential that we run a few more tests to rule out certain conditions. I understand your frustration, but please know that we're here to help, and we won't rest until we have a clearer picture of your husband's condition."

Mrs. Johnson's demeanor softened slightly as she realized that Dr. Smith was genuinely invested in her husband's well-being. "I... I appreciate your efforts, Dr. Smith," she admitted hesitantly.

"I'm just scared, you know? Not knowing what's wrong with him is driving me crazy."

Dr. Smith nodded sympathetically. "I completely understand, Mrs. Johnson. It's perfectly normal to feel scared and frustrated in a situation like this. But please know that you're not alone. We're here to support both you and your husband every step of the way."

As the conversation drew to a close, Dr. Smith made sure to address Mrs. Johnson's concerns about communication breakdowns and reassure her that he would keep her informed of any developments in her husband's care.

"Thank you for taking the time to speak with me, Mrs. Johnson," Dr. Smith said warmly. "I'll personally oversee your husband's care from here on out, and I promise to keep you updated every step of the way. If you have any questions or concerns, please don't hesitate to reach out." Mrs. Johnson nodded gratefully, her demeanor noticeably lighter than before. "Thank you, Dr.

Smith," she said sincerely. "I appreciate your understanding and support."

As Dr. Smith watched Mrs. Johnson leave the emergency room, he couldn't help but feel a sense of satisfaction. By avoiding common communication traps and employing effective strategies, he had managed to diffuse a tense situation and reassure a worried relative. And most importantly, he had reaffirmed his commitment to providing compassionate care to his patients and their families.

In the described, Dr. Smith effectively utilized several strategies from the list provided to navigate the conversation with Mrs. Johnson:

1. Avoiding Obvious Traps:

Silence or Violence: Dr. Smith avoided reacting defensively or engaging in a shouting match with Mrs. Johnson, which could have escalated the situation.

Making Assumptions: Instead of assuming Mrs. Johnson's intentions or emotions, Dr. Smith actively listened to her concerns and gathered more information.

Righteousness: Dr. Smith prioritized understanding Mrs. Johnson's perspective and providing support rather than proving himself right.

Avoiding the Fool's Choice: Dr. Smith demonstrated that it's possible to maintain honesty while still preserving the doctor-patient relationship by promising to keep Mrs. Johnson informed.

2. Choosing the Best Strategy:

Ask for Others' Paths: Dr. Smith encouraged Mrs. Johnson to share her husband's symptoms and concerns, demonstrating his willingness to understand her perspective.

Make It Safe: By remaining calm and empathetic, Dr. Smith created a safe environment for Mrs. Johnson to express her frustrations and fears.

Master My Stories: Dr. Smith challenged any unhelpful narratives or assumptions by actively listening to Mrs. Johnson's story and refraining from jumping to conclusions.

STATE My Path: Dr. Smith confidently and skillfully shared his perspective by reassuring Mrs. Johnson of the medical team's commitment to her husband's care and promising to keep her informed.

Overall, Dr. Smith's approach was characterized by empathy, active listening, and a commitment to maintaining open communication with Mrs. Johnson. By avoiding common communication traps and choosing effective strategies, he successfully diffused a tense situation and reassured Mrs. Johnson of her husband's care.

Appropriate Diagnosis is Not Being Made: -
"The Diagnostic Path: Navigating Communication"
Characters:

- Dr. Nayana Deb (Doctor)
- Mr. Arjun Mehta (Patient)

Scene: A Doctor's Office

(The scene opens with Mr. Mehta seated in the consultation room, looking concerned but calm. Dr. Deb enters, carrying a clipboard with his test results.)

Dr. Deb: Good morning, Mr. Mehta. Thank you for your patience as we've worked through some tests. I understand it's been a bit of a process, and I'd like to address your concerns today.

Mr. Mehta: Good morning, doctor. Honestly, I'm feeling a little frustrated. It's been weeks, and I still don't know what's wrong. Is this delay normal?

Dr. Deb: That's completely understandable, Mr. Mehta. Let me explain the diagnostic process so you can see why it sometimes takes time. Diagnosing a condition is a bit like solving a puzzle—we gather pieces of information from your symptoms, test results, and medical history to get the full picture.

Mr. Mehta *(leans forward)*: So, it's not just about running more tests?

Dr. Deb: Exactly. Each test has a specific purpose. For instance, we started with blood work to check for common markers of inflammation or infection. When that didn't explain all your symptoms, we moved to imaging to see if there was anything structural, like an issue with your organs. Now, based on those results, we're focusing on more targeted tests to pinpoint the root cause.

Mr. Mehta *(nodding slowly)*: I see. But why not just run all the tests at once? Wouldn't that save time?

Dr. Deb: That's a fair question. Running all tests upfront can lead to unnecessary expenses and sometimes false positives, which create more confusion. It's better to start with broad strokes and narrow down. Plus, we prioritize your safety—some tests, like invasive procedures, carry risks, so we only do them when absolutely necessary.

Mr. Mehta: I hadn't thought of that. But why do I feel like progress is so slow?

Dr. Deb *(pauses thoughtfully)*: That's a valid feeling. It might seem slow because we're taking a careful, step-by-step approach to avoid missing anything critical. This ensures the diagnosis we give is as accurate as possible. Also, remember, healing is not just about knowing the problem—it's about understanding it well enough to treat it effectively.

Mr. Mehta *(relaxes a bit)*: That makes sense. What's next, then?

Dr. Deb: Next, we're focusing on [specific upcoming test], which will help us confirm or rule out [condition]. If that test is inconclusive, we have a few more options to explore.

Mr. Mehta: And what if you don't find anything?

Dr. Deb *(smiling warmly)*: That's always a possibility, but it doesn't mean there's no issue—it might just be something rare or subtle. In that case, we'll discuss more advanced diagnostic techniques or consult with specialists.

Mr. Mehta *(after a moment's pause)*: I appreciate the clarity, doctor. It feels better knowing there's a plan.

Dr. Deb: I'm glad to hear that. Communication is key. If you ever feel uncertain or need clarification, please don't hesitate to ask. We're in this together.

(Dr. Deb places a reassuring hand on Mr. Mehta's file and smiles warmly. Mr. Mehta looks more at ease as the scene closes.)

Communication Analysis:

- Avoiding Silence or Violence: Dr. Deb maintains a calm, empathetic tone, addressing Mr. Mehta's frustration without dismissing or reacting defensively.
- No Labeling or Stereotyping: Dr. Deb treats Mr. Mehta's concerns as valid and doesn't assume he's impatient or demanding.
- Staying on Topic: The conversation remains focused on explaining the diagnostic process and alleviating concerns.
- Avoiding False Dilemmas: Dr. Deb explains why not all tests are done at once and provides a clear rationale for the step-by-step approach.
- Prioritizing Resolution: The dialogue ends with a clear plan, ensuring Mr. Mehta feels heard and reassured

4.Irrelevant investigations are being ordered

In the bustling emergency room, Dr. Patel found herself facing an irate relative, Mr. Thompson, whose elderly mother was admitted earlier that day. Mr. Thompson's frustration was palpable as he launched into a tirade against the medical staff.
Mr. Thompson's voice rose with anger, "I've had enough of your so-called 'investigations'! All you care about is keeping my mother here longer and racking up the bills!"
Dr. Patel took a deep breath, reminding herself of the strategies she had learned to navigate such challenging conversations. She recognized the need to avoid falling into common traps that could escalate the situation further.
"Mr. Thompson, I understand that you're feeling frustrated right now," Dr. Patel began calmly, acknowledging his concerns without dismissing them.
"You bet I'm frustrated!" Mr. Thompson interjected. "My mother has been poked and prodded all day, and we still don't have any answers!"
Dr. Patel made a conscious effort to avoid the trap of labeling or stereotyping Mr. Thompson's emotions. Instead, she focused on addressing his underlying fears and doubts. "I can imagine how difficult this must be for you and your family," Dr. Patel replied empathetically. "Our priority is to provide the best possible care for your mother, and sometimes that does require

conducting additional tests to ensure we have a clear understanding of her condition. Similarly these tests guide us in deciding the next line of management as well and improvement in clinical parameters provide hope for clinical improvement."

Mr. Thompson's expression softened slightly, but he remained skeptical. "I don't buy it," he retorted. "You doctors are just trying to cover your backsides and milk us for every penny we've got!"

Dr. Patel recognized the need to maintain a safe environment for dialogue, even in the face of Mr. Thompson's hostility. She chose her words carefully, aiming to address his concerns while also asserting the integrity of the medical team's actions.

"I can assure you, Mr. Thompson, that every decision we make here is in the best interest of your mother's health," Dr. Patel stated firmly. "But I understand that you may have doubts, and I'm here to address them to the best of my ability."

Mr. Thompson's demeanor softened further as Dr. Patel's words began to resonate with him. Sensing an opportunity to foster open dialogue, Dr. Patel encouraged Mr. Thompson to share his perspective.

"Mr. Thompson, I want to understand your concerns better," Dr. Patel said gently. "Can you tell me more about what you're feeling right now?"

As Mr. Thompson opened up about his fears for his mother's well-being and his frustration with the healthcare system, Dr. Patel listened attentively, making sure to avoid making assumptions or judgments.He was not judgmental and explained the situation clearly.

Once Mr. Thompson had finished speaking, Dr. Patel took a moment to summarize his concerns, validating his feelings and addressing each point with empathy and understanding.

"Thank you for sharing that with me, Mr. Thompson," Dr. Patel said sincerely. "I want to assure you that we're here to support you and your mother every step of the way. Let's work together to ensure she receives the care she needs."

By avoiding common communication traps and choosing effective strategies, Dr. Patel had successfully navigated a challenging conversation with Mr. Thompson. Through empathy, active listening, and open dialogue, she had fostered understanding and trust, ultimately strengthening the doctor-patient relationship.

In the described, Dr. Patel effectively employed several strategies from the list provided to address Mr. Thompson's aggressive and accusatory behavior:

1. Avoiding Obvious Traps:

-       Silence or Violence: Dr. Patel avoided responding defensively or engaging in a verbal confrontation with Mr. Thompson, thereby preventing the situation from escalating. - Labeling and Stereotyping: Instead of dismissing Mr. Thompson's concerns or labeling him as unreasonable, Dr. Patel acknowledged his feelings and focused on understanding his perspective.

-        Making Assumptions: Dr. Patel avoided assuming Mr. Thompson's motives or intentions behind his accusations and instead sought clarity through open dialogue.

-        Righteousness: Dr. Patel prioritized finding common ground and mutual understanding over proving herself right or defending the medical team's actions.

-        The Blame Game: Instead of blaming Mr. Thompson for his behavior or dismissing his concerns, Dr. Patel emphasized shared responsibility in addressing his doubts and fears.

2. Choosing the Best Strategy:

Ask for Others' Paths: Dr. Patel encouraged Mr. Thompson to share his perspective and concerns, demonstrating her willingness to understand his viewpoint.

Make It Safe: By acknowledging Mr. Thompson's frustrations and validating his feelings, Dr. Patel created a safe environment for dialogue, encouraging honesty and openness. - Master

My Stories: Dr. Patel challenged any unhelpful narratives or assumptions by actively listening to Mr. Thompson's story and refraining from jumping to conclusions about his motives or intentions.

STATE My Path: Dr. Patel confidently and skillfully shared her perspective by reassuring Mr. Thompson of the medical team's commitment to his mother's well-being and addressing his concerns with empathy and understanding.

Overall, Dr. Patel's approach was characterized by empathy, active listening, and a commitment to maintaining open communication with Mr. Thompson. By avoiding common communication traps and choosing effective strategies, she successfully diffused a tense situation and fostered understanding and trust, ultimately strengthening the doctor-patient relationship.

5.Too much of Costly medicines are being used

In a bustling hospital corridor, Dr. Lee found herself confronted by a visibly agitated Mr. Davis, whose elderly mother was admitted for treatment. Mr. Davis was fuming with frustration about the medication regimen prescribed for his mother and didn't hesitate to express his grievances. Mr. Davis exclaimed, "Doctor, I've had it with these expensive medications you keep pumping into my mother! It's draining our savings, and I'm not convinced she needs all of them!" Dr. Lee took a deep breath, remembering the importance of avoiding common communication traps in such challenging situations. She recognized the need to address Mr. Davis's concerns with empathy and understanding.
"Mr. Davis, I understand your concerns about the medications," Dr. Lee replied calmly, acknowledging his frustrations without dismissing them.
"You bet I'm concerned!" Mr. Davis retorted. "Every time I check the bill, it seems like there's another expensive drug added to the list!"
Dr. Lee avoided the trap of assuming Mr. Davis's intentions or motives behind his accusations.
Instead, she focused on understanding his perspective and addressing his doubts.
"I can appreciate how overwhelming this must feel for you," Dr. Lee responded, choosing her words carefully. "Our priority is always to provide the best possible care for your mother, and sometimes that does involve using certain medications to manage her condition

effectively." Mr. Davis's expression remained skeptical, but Dr. Lee continued to maintain a safe environment for dialogue, encouraging him to share his perspective.

"Mr. Davis, I want to understand your concerns better," Dr. Lee said gently. "Can you tell me more about what you're feeling right now?"

As Mr. Davis opened up about his worries regarding the financial strain and his doubts about the necessity of certain medications, Dr. Lee listened attentively, refraining from making judgments or assumptions. Once Mr. Davis had finished speaking, Dr. Lee took a moment to summarize his concerns, validating his feelings and addressing each point with empathy and understanding.

"Thank you for sharing that with me, Mr. Davis," Dr. Lee said sincerely. "I want you to know that we're here to support both you and your mother throughout her treatment journey. Let's work together to find a solution that addresses your concerns while ensuring your mother receives the care she needs."

"We always keep early and speedy recovery of our patients on priority and for that sometimes we need costly medicines."

By avoiding common communication traps and choosing effective strategies, Dr. Lee successfully navigated a challenging conversation with Mr. Davis. Through empathy, active listening, and open dialogue, she fostered understanding and trust, ultimately strengthening the doctor-patient relationship.

let's break down how Dr. Lee applied different strategies in her conversation with Mr. Davis:

1. Avoiding Obvious Traps:

Silence or Violence: Dr. Lee avoided responding defensively or engaging in a verbal confrontation with Mr. Davis, which could have escalated the situation.

Making Assumptions: Dr. Lee refrained from assuming Mr. Davis's motives behind his accusations and instead sought clarity through open dialogue.

Righteousness: Dr. Lee prioritized finding common ground and mutual understanding over proving herself right or defending the prescribed medication regimen.

The Blame Game: Instead of blaming Mr. Davis for his concerns or dismissing them, Dr.

Lee emphasized shared responsibility in addressing his doubts and fears.

2. Choosing the Best Strategy:

Ask for Others' Paths: Dr. Lee encouraged Mr. Davis to share his perspective and concerns, demonstrating her willingness to understand his viewpoint.

Make It Safe: By acknowledging Mr. Davis's frustrations and validating his feelings, Dr.

Lee created a safe environment for dialogue, encouraging honesty and openness. -   Master My Stories: Dr. Lee challenged any unhelpful narratives or assumptions by actively listening to Mr. Davis's story and refraining from jumping to conclusions about his motives or intentions.

STATE My Path: Dr. Lee confidently and skillfully shared her perspective by reassuring Mr. Davis of the medical team's commitment to his mother's well-being and addressing his concerns with empathy and understanding.

Overall, Dr. Lee's approach was characterized by empathy, active listening, and a commitment to maintaining open communication with Mr. Davis.

By avoiding common communication traps and choosing effective strategies, she successfully diffused a tense situation and fostered understanding and trust, ultimately strengthening the doctor-patient relationship.

6.Patient is not improving ,ICU stay is prolonged

In the busy hospital ward, Dr. Rodriguez found herself facing a confrontational relative, Mrs. Thompson, whose husband had been admitted for treatment. Mrs. Thompson's frustration was evident as she launched into a tirade against the medical staff.
Mrs. Thompson's voice trembled with anger, "Doctor, what's going on? My husband has been here for days, and he's not getting any better! What are you doing about it?" Dr. Rodriguez took a deep breath, reminding herself of the importance of effective communication in such situations. She recognized the need to navigate Mrs. Thompson's concerns with empathy and understanding, while also addressing the core issue at hand.

"Mrs. Thompson, I understand your concerns about your husband's condition," Dr. Rodriguez responded calmly, acknowledging Mrs. Thompson's emotions without escalating the situation.
Mrs. Thompson's frustration boiled over as she continued, "I don't think you understand at all! We've been waiting for answers, and all we get are excuses and delays!"
Dr. Rodriguez consciously avoided the trap of assuming Mrs. Thompson's motives or intentions behind her accusations. Instead, she focused on understanding Mrs. Thompson's perspective and addressing her doubts.

"I can imagine how overwhelming this must feel for you," Dr. Rodriguez replied, choosing her words carefully. "Our priority is to provide the best possible care for your husband, and I want to assure you that we're doing everything we can to help him improve." Mrs. Thompson's expression remained skeptical, but Dr. Rodriguez persisted in creating a safe environment for dialogue.

"Mrs. Thompson, I want to understand your concerns better," Dr. Rodriguez said gently. "Can you tell me more about what you're feeling right now?" As Mrs. Thompson opened up about her fears for her husband's health and her frustrations with the lack of progress, Dr. Rodriguez listened attentively, refraining from making judgments or assumptions. Once Mrs. Thompson had finished speaking, Dr. Rodriguez took a moment to summarize her concerns, validating her feelings and addressing each point with empathy and understanding.

"Thank you for sharing that with me, Mrs. Thompson," Dr. Rodriguez said sincerely. "I want you to know that we're here to support both you and your husband throughout his treatment journey. Many of the times in critically ill patients its not easy to figure out the outcomes and such situations may not be rewarding in some cases. Let's work together to find a solution that addresses your concerns while ensuring your husband receives the care he needs."

By avoiding common communication traps and choosing effective strategies, Dr. Rodriguez successfully diffused a tense situation and fostered understanding and trust, ultimately strengthening the doctor-patient relationship.

Let's break down how Dr. Rodriguez applied different strategies in her conversation with Mrs. Thompson:

1. Avoiding Obvious Traps:

- Silence or Violence: Dr. Rodriguez avoided responding defensively or engaging in a verbal confrontation with Mrs. Thompson, which could have escalated the situation.

- Making Assumptions: Dr. Rodriguez refrained from assuming Mrs. Thompson's motives behind her accusations and instead sought clarity through open dialogue.

- Righteousness: Dr. Rodriguez prioritized finding common ground and mutual understanding over proving herself right or defending the medical team's actions.

- The Blame Game: Instead of blaming Mrs. Thompson for her concerns or dismissing them, Dr. Rodriguez emphasized shared responsibility in addressing her doubts and fears.

2. Choosing the Best Strategy:

- Ask for Others' Paths: Dr. Rodriguez encouraged Mrs. Thompson to share her perspective and concerns, demonstrating her willingness to understand her viewpoint.

- Make It Safe: By acknowledging Mrs. Thompson's frustrations and validating her feelings, Dr. Rodriguez created a safe environment for dialogue, encouraging honesty and openness. - Master My Stories: Dr. Rodriguez challenged any unhelpful narratives or assumptions by actively listening to Mrs. Thompson's story and refraining from jumping to conclusions about her motives or intentions.

- STATE My Path: Dr. Rodriguez confidently and skillfully shared her perspective by reassuring Mrs. Thompson of the medical team's commitment to her husband's well-being and addressing her concerns with empathy and understanding.

Overall, Dr. Rodriguez's approach was characterized by empathy, active listening, and a commitment to maintaining open communication with Mrs. Thompson. By avoiding common communication traps and choosing effective strategies, she successfully diffused a tense situation and fostered understanding and trust, ultimately strengthening the doctor-patient relationship.

7.Apprpriate Communication with relatives is not being made.

In the bustling hospital hallway, Dr. Thompson found himself facing an irate relative, Mrs. Johnson, whose daughter was undergoing treatment. Mrs. Johnson's frustration was evident as she voiced her concerns about the lack of communication from the medical team.

Mrs. Johnson's voice trembled with anger, "Doctor, I've had it with the lack of communication from this hospital! We have no idea what's going on with our daughter's treatment, and it's unacceptable!"

Dr. Thompson took a deep breath, reminding himself of the importance of effective communication in such situations. He recognized the need to navigate Mrs. Johnson's concerns with empathy and understanding, while also addressing the core issue at hand.

"Mrs. Johnson, I understand your concerns about the communication regarding your daughter's treatment," Dr. Thompson replied calmly, acknowledging Mrs. Johnson's emotions without escalating the situation.

Mrs. Johnson's frustration boiled over as she continued, "We've been left in the dark for too long! We deserve to know what's happening with our daughter's care!"

Dr. Thompson consciously avoided the trap of assuming Mrs. Johnson's motives or intentions behind her accusations. Instead, he focused on understanding Mrs. Johnson's perspective and addressing her doubts.

"I can imagine how overwhelming this must feel for you," Dr. Thompson responded, choosing his words carefully. "Our priority is to provide the best possible care for your daughter, and I want to assure you that we are committed to keeping you informed every step of the way." Mrs. Johnson's expression remained skeptical, but Dr. Thompson persisted in creating a safe environment for dialogue.

"Mrs. Johnson, I want to understand your concerns better," Dr. Thompson said gently. "Can you tell me more about what you're feeling right now?"

As Mrs. Johnson opened up about her fears for her daughter's health and her frustrations with the lack of communication, Dr. Thompson listened attentively, refraining from making judgments or assumptions. Once Mrs. Johnson had finished speaking, Dr. Thompson took a moment to summarize her concerns, validating her feelings and addressing each point with empathy and understanding. "Thank you for sharing that with me, Mrs. Johnson," Dr. Thompson said sincerely. "I want you to know that we're here to support both you and your daughter throughout her treatment journey. Let's work together to find a solution that addresses your concerns while ensuring your daughter receives the care she needs."

By avoiding common communication traps and choosing effective strategies, Dr. Thompson successfully diffused a tense situation and fostered understanding and trust, ultimately strengthening the doctor-patient relationship.

Let's examine how Dr. Thompson applied different strategies in his conversation with Mrs. Johnson:

1 A.Avoiding Obvious Traps

Silence

Dr. Thompson avoided responding defensively or engaging in a verbal confrontation with Mrs. Johnson, maintaining a calm demeanor despite her frustration.

Making Assumptions

Dr. Thompson refrained from assuming Mrs. Johnson's motives or intentions behind her accusations and instead sought clarification through open dialogue.

Righteousness

Dr. Thompson prioritized understanding Mrs. Johnson's perspective and addressing her concerns rather than focusing on proving himself or the medical team right.

The Blame Game

Instead of blaming Mrs. Johnson for her frustrations or dismissing her concerns, Dr. Thompson emphasized shared responsibility in ensuring effective communication.

2.Choosing the Best Strategy

Ask for Others' Paths

Dr. Thompson encouraged Mrs. Johnson to share her perspective and concerns, demonstrating his willingness to understand her viewpoint.

Make It Safe

 By acknowledging Mrs. Johnson's frustrations and validating her feelings, Dr. Thompson created a safe environment for dialogue, encouraging honesty and openness.

Master My Stories

Dr. Thompson actively listened to Mrs. Johnson's story and refrained from making assumptions or judgments about her experiences or intentions.

STATE My Path

Dr. Thompson confidently and skillfully shared his perspective by reassuring Mrs. Johnson of the medical team's commitment to her daughter's well-being and addressing her concerns with empathy and understanding. Overall, Dr. Thompson's approach was characterized by empathy, active listening, and a commitment to maintaining open communication with Mrs. Johnson. By avoiding common communication traps and choosing effective strategies, he successfully diffused a tense situation and fostered understanding and trust, ultimately strengthening the doctor-patient relationship.

8.Relatives are Not allowed to see their patients frequently

In the busy hospital corridor, Dr. Ramirez found herself facing an irate relative, Mrs. Collins, whose loved one was undergoing treatment. Mrs.
Collins's frustration was evident as she voiced her concerns about the limited access to her family member.
Mrs. Collins's voice trembled with anger, "Doctor, why are you restricting our visits with our family member? We should be allowed to see them whenever we want!"
Dr. Ramirez took a deep breath, understanding the importance of effective communication in such situations. She acknowledged Mrs. Collins's concerns while remaining composed. "Mrs. Collins, I hear your frustration about the visitation restrictions," Dr. Ramirez responded calmly, avoiding escalating the tension.
Mrs. Collins's frustration mounted as she continued, "This is unacceptable! We have the right to be with our family member whenever we choose!"
Dr. Ramirez consciously avoided jumping to conclusions about Mrs. Collins's intentions. Instead, she focused on understanding Mrs. Collins's perspective and addressing her concerns. "I understand that this is challenging for you," Dr. Ramirez replied empathetically. "Our top priority is the well-being and safety of your family member, and sometimes visitation restrictions are necessary to support their recovery."

Mrs. Collins's expression remained skeptical, but Dr. Ramirez persisted in creating a safe environment for dialogue.

"Mrs. Collins, I want to understand your concerns better," Dr. Ramirez said gently. "Could you share more about what you're feeling right now?"

As Mrs. Collins opened up about her fears and frustrations, Dr. Ramirez listened attentively, refraining from making assumptions.

Once Mrs. Collins had finished speaking, Dr. Ramirez summarized her concerns, validating her feelings and addressing each point with empathy and understanding.

"Thank you for sharing your thoughts with me, Mrs. Collins," Dr. Ramirez said sincerely. "I want you to know that we're here to support both you and your family member throughout their treatment. Let's work together to find a solution that ensures their safety while also addressing your need for connection."

By avoiding common communication traps and choosing effective strategies, Dr. Ramirez successfully diffused the tense situation and fostered understanding and trust, ultimately strengthening the doctor-relative relationship.

Let's analyze how Dr. Ramirez applied different strategies in her conversation with Mrs. Collins:

1. Avoiding Obvious Traps

Silence or Violence : Dr. Ramirez maintained a calm and composed demeanor, avoiding responding defensively or engaging in a verbal confrontation with Mrs. Collins, which could escalate the situation.

-Making Assumptions

: Instead of assuming Mrs. Collins's intentions or motives behind her accusations, Dr. Ramirez focused on understanding her perspective and addressing her concerns directly.

-

Righteousness: Dr. Ramirez prioritized understanding Mrs. Collins's emotions and concerns over proving herself right or defending the hospital's policies.

-The Blame Game: Rather than blaming Mrs. Collins for her frustrations, Dr. Ramirez acknowledged her concerns and emphasized shared responsibility in ensuring the well-being of her family member.

2.Choosing the Best Strategy

:Ask for Others' Paths: Dr. Ramirez encouraged Mrs. Collins to share her perspective and concerns, demonstrating her willingness to understand her viewpoint.

Make It Safe : By acknowledging Mrs. Collins's frustrations and validating her feelings, Dr. Ramirez created a safe environment for dialogue, fostering honesty and openness. Master My Stories: Dr. Ramirez actively listened to Mrs. Collins's story without making assumptions or judgments, recognizing the importance of understanding her narrative.

STATE My Path : Dr. Ramirez confidently and skillfully shared her perspective on the visitation restrictions, reassuring Mrs. Collins of the hospital's commitment to her family member's wellbeing while also addressing her need for connection. Overall, Dr. Ramirez's approach was characterized by empathy, active listening, and a commitment to maintaining open communication with Mrs.
Collins. By avoiding common communication traps and choosing effective strategies, she successfully diffused a tense situation and fostered understanding and trust, ultimately strengthening the doctor-relative relationship.

9.Patient is not getting adequate Food and water

In the dimly lit hospital room, Dr. Garcia walked in to check on her patient, only to be met with tear-filled eyes and trembling hands of Mrs. Thompson, the patient's daughter. It was evident that something troubled her deeply.

Dr. Garcia approached Mrs. Thompson with a gentle smile, but her heart sank as she noticed the distress etched on her face. "Mrs. Thompson, how can I help you today?" Dr. Garcia asked, her voice filled with concern.

Tears welled up in Mrs. Thompson's eyes as she spoke, her voice quivering with emotion. "Doctor, I'm deeply worried about my mother. She's not getting enough food and water here. I can see her getting weaker every day, and it breaks my heart."

Dr. Garcia's heart ached as she listened to Mrs. Thompson's heartfelt plea. She knew that adequate nutrition and hydration were crucial for her patient's recovery, and she shared Mrs. Thompson's concerns.

"I understand how difficult this must be for you, Mrs. Thompson," Dr. Garcia said softly, placing a comforting hand on her shoulder. "Your mother's well-being is our top priority, and I assure you that we'll do everything we can to address this issue."

Mrs. Thompson wiped away her tears, her eyes searching for reassurance. "But it's been days since she's had a proper meal, and she's barely drinking any water," she whispered, her voice trembling with fear.

Dr. Garcia took a moment to gather her thoughts, her heart heavy with empathy for Mrs. Thompson's anguish. She knew that swift action was needed to ensure her patient's needs were met.

"Mrs. Thompson, I want to assure you that we'll work together to resolve this immediately," Dr. Garcia said with determination. "I'll personally speak to the nursing staff and ensure that your mother receives the nourishment and hydration she needs to recover."

Tears of relief streamed down Mrs. Thompson's face as she embraced Dr. Garcia tightly, her gratitude palpable. "Thank you, Doctor. Knowing that you're here for us gives me hope," she whispered, her voice filled with gratitude.

Dr. Garcia held Mrs. Thompson's hand, offering her a reassuring smile. "We're in this together, Mrs. Thompson. Your mother is in good hands, and we'll do everything in our power to help her get better," she said with conviction.

As Dr. Garcia left the room, her heart swelled with compassion for her patient and her family. She knew that providing comfort and support during moments of distress was just as important as medical treatment. And with Mrs. Thompson's trust in her, she was more determined than ever to ensure her patient's well-being, one compassionate gesture at a time.

Let's break down the strategies used by Dr. Garcia in each step of the conversation:

1. Avoiding Obvious Traps:

-        Silence or Violence: Dr. Garcia approached Mrs. Thompson with a gentle smile, avoiding any confrontational or aggressive behavior, which could have escalated the situation. - Making Assumptions: Instead of assuming Mrs. Thompson's concerns were unfounded, Dr. Garcia listened attentively to her and validated her emotions without judgment.

-        Avoiding the Issue: Dr. Garcia didn't deflect or ignore Mrs. Thompson's concerns about her mother's inadequate nutrition and hydration. She addressed the issue head-on, acknowledging its importance.

-        Righteousness: Dr. Garcia empathized with Mrs. Thompson's distress, demonstrating humility and understanding rather than asserting her authority as a doctor.

-        The Blame Game: Rather than blaming Mrs. Thompson for her concerns or making excuses, Dr. Garcia assured her that they would work together to find a solution, fostering collaboration and trust.

2. Choosing the Best Strategy:

-        Ask for Others' Paths: Dr. Garcia actively listened to Mrs. Thompson's concerns, asking openended questions to understand her perspective better and encourage dialogue.

-        Make It Safe: By offering comfort and reassurance, Dr. Garcia created a safe environment for

Mrs. Thompson to express her worries openly, fostering honesty and openness in their conversation.

-        Master My Stories: Dr. Garcia recognized the emotional impact of Mrs. Thompson's concerns and responded with empathy and compassion, acknowledging the gravity of the situation. - STATE My Path: Dr. Garcia shared her plan of action with Mrs. Thompson confidently and assuredly, reassuring her that they would address the issue promptly and effectively. Overall, Dr. Garcia's approach was characterized by empathy, active listening, and a commitment to addressing Mrs. Thompson's concerns with compassion and understanding. By avoiding common communication traps and choosing effective strategies, she successfully diffused a tense situation and fostered trust and collaboration with Mrs. Thompson, ultimately strengthening their doctor-patient relationship.

10.Diaper change is not done on time

In the bustling neonatal intensive care unit, Dr. Patel approached the worried parents of a premature baby, who looked visibly distressed. Mrs.
Johnson's eyes welled up with tears as she spoke, her voice trembling with concern.
"Doctor, we've noticed that the diaper changes for our baby aren't happening on time," Mrs.
Johnson said, her voice filled with worry.
Dr. Patel's heart sank as she listened to Mrs. Johnson's distress. She knew how crucial timely diaper changes were for preventing infections and ensuring the baby's comfort.
"I'm so sorry to hear that, Mrs. Johnson," Dr. Patel replied, her tone gentle and empathetic. "Your baby's well-being is our top priority, and I
understand how important it is for diaper changes to be done promptly."
Mrs. Johnson wiped away her tears, her anxiety evident in her voice. "It's just that we've noticed delays multiple times, and it worries us," she said, her voice quivering with emotion.
Dr. Patel took a deep breath, her mind racing with solutions to address the issue. She knew that open communication and swift action were essential in such situations.
"I completely understand your concerns, Mrs. Johnson," Dr. Patel replied, her voice filled with reassurance. "I'll

personally speak to the nursing staff and ensure that diaper changes are prioritized for your baby."

Tears of relief filled Mrs. Johnson's eyes as she embraced Dr. Patel tightly, her gratitude palpable. "Thank you, Doctor. Knowing that you're here for our baby means the world to us," she whispered, her voice filled with gratitude.

Dr. Patel smiled warmly, her heart swelling with compassion for the worried parents. "We're all here to support you and your baby every step of the way," she said with conviction. "Your baby is in good hands, and we'll do everything we can to ensure their comfort and wellbeing."

As Dr. Patel left the room, she made a mental note to address the issue with the nursing staff promptly. She knew that providing timely and

compassionate care was essential for the health and happiness of their little patient. And with Mrs. Johnson's trust in her, she was more determined than ever to ensure that every aspect of their baby's care was handled with the utmost diligence and compassion.

Let's break down the strategies employed by Dr. Patel in each step of the conversation:

1.Avoiding Obvious Traps

: Silence or Violence: Dr. Patel approached Mrs. Johnson with a calm and empathetic demeanor, avoiding any confrontational or defensive responses that could escalate the situation. -Making Assumptions: Rather than dismissing Mrs. Johnson's concerns or assuming they were unfounded, Dr. Patel actively listened to her and validated her emotions without judgment.

-

Avoiding the Issue : Dr. Patel didn't deflect or ignore Mrs. Johnson's concerns about the delayed diaper changes. Instead, she addressed the issue directly, acknowledging its importance. -Righteousness : Dr. Patel empathized with Mrs. Johnson's distress, demonstrating humility and understanding rather than asserting her authority as a doctor.

The Blame Game: Instead of blaming Mrs. Johnson for her worries or making excuses, Dr. Patel assured her that they would work together to find a solution, fostering collaboration and trust. 2.Choosing the Best Strategy :Ask for Others' Paths: Dr. Patel actively listened to Mrs. Johnson's concerns, asking open-ended questions to understand her perspective better and encourage dialogue.

-Make It Safe : By offering comfort and reassurance, Dr. Patel created a safe environment for Mrs. Johnson to express her worries openly, fostering honesty and openness in their conversation.

-Master My Stories: Dr. Patel recognized the emotional impact of Mrs. Johnson's concerns and responded with empathy and compassion, acknowledging the gravity of the situation. -STATE My Path: Dr. Patel shared her plan of action with Mrs. Johnson confidently and assuredly,

reassuring her that they would address the issue
promptly and effectively.

Overall, Dr. Patel's approach was characterized by
empathy, active listening, and a commitment to
addressing Mrs. Johnson's concerns with compassion
and understanding. By avoiding common
communication traps and choosing effective strategies,
she successfully diffused a tense situation and fostered
trust and collaboration with Mrs. Johnson, ultimately
strengthening their doctor-patient relationship.

11.Doctor is giving False hope about the patient

In the sterile confines of the hospital corridor, Dr. Rivera found herself face to face with Mr. and Mrs. Thompson, their expressions wrought with anxiety and desperation. Mrs. Thompson's eyes glistened with unshed tears as she voiced her deepest fear.

"Doctor, we feel like you're giving us false hope about our daughter's condition," Mrs. Thompson whispered, her voice heavy with emotion.

Dr. Rivera's heart clenched at the accusation, knowing the weight of their anguish. She had been tirelessly working to provide comfort and care, but the fear of disappointing the family weighed heavily on her shoulders.

"I understand how difficult this must be for you, Mrs. Thompson," Dr. Rivera responded softly, her tone laced with empathy. "Believe me, I would never want to give you false hope. I'm here to support you through every step of your daughter's journey."

Mrs. Thompson's shoulders slumped with the weight of her worry, her voice trembling as she continued, "It's just that... we're afraid of being let down again. We need to know the truth, even if it's hard to hear."

Dr. Rivera took a deep breath, her mind racing with the complexity of their situation. She knew that honesty was paramount, even in the face of uncertainty.

"I hear your concerns, Mrs. Thompson," Dr. Rivera replied, her voice steady despite the turmoil in her heart. "I promise to always be honest with you about your daughter's condition. Let's work together to navigate this difficult journey, one step at a time." Tears welled up in Mrs. Thompson's eyes as she reached out to grasp Dr. Rivera's hand, her gratitude palpable. "Thank you, Doctor. Knowing that we can trust you means everything to us," she whispered, her voice filled with emotion.

Dr. Rivera offered a reassuring smile, her determination unwavering. "We're in this together, Mrs. Thompson," she said with conviction. "Your daughter is receiving the best possible care, and we'll do everything in our power to support her and your family."

As Dr. Rivera walked away, she carried the weight of their trust on her shoulders, knowing that their journey ahead would be filled with challenges and uncertainty. But with their trust in her, she felt a renewed sense of purpose, ready to face whatever lay ahead with honesty, compassion, and unwavering dedication.

Let's analyze the strategies employed by Dr. Rivera in each step of the conversation:

1. Avoiding Obvious Traps:

-        Silence or Violence: Dr. Rivera approached the Thompsons with a calm and empathetic demeanor, avoiding any defensive or confrontational responses that could escalate the situation.

-        Making Assumptions: Instead of dismissing Mrs. Thompson's concerns or assuming they were unfounded, Dr. Rivera actively listened to her and validated her emotions without judgment. - Avoiding the Issue: Dr. Rivera didn't deflect or ignore Mrs. Thompson's concerns about false hope. Instead, she addressed the issue directly, acknowledging its importance. -   Righteousness: Dr. Rivera empathized with Mrs. Thompson's distress, demonstrating humility and understanding rather than asserting her authority as a doctor.

-	The Blame Game: Instead of blaming Mrs. Thompson for her worries or making excuses, Dr. Rivera assured her that they would work together to find a solution, fostering collaboration and trust.

2. Choosing the Best Strategy:

-	Ask for Others' Paths: Dr. Rivera actively listened to Mrs. Thompson's concerns, asking openended questions to understand her perspective better and encourage dialogue.

-	Make It Safe: By offering comfort and reassurance, Dr. Rivera created a safe environment for Mrs. Thompson to express her worries openly, fostering honesty and openness in their conversation.

-	Master My Stories: Dr. Rivera recognized the emotional impact of Mrs. Thompson's concerns and responded with empathy and compassion, acknowledging the gravity of the situation. - STATE My Path: Dr. Rivera shared her plan of action with Mrs. Thompson confidently and assuredly, reassuring her that they would address the issue of false hope promptly and effectively.

Overall, Dr. Rivera's approach was characterized by empathy, active listening, and a commitment to addressing Mrs. Thompson's concerns with compassion and understanding. By avoiding common communication traps and choosing effective strategies, she successfully diffused a tense situation and fostered trust and collaboration with Mrs. Thompson, ultimately strengthening their doctor-patient relationship.

12.Patient was better but Doctor's Intervention made it worse.

In the dimly lit waiting room of the hospital, Dr. Mitchell braced herself as Mr. and Mrs. Rodriguez stormed in, their faces contorted with rage and frustration. Mrs. Rodriguez's voice pierced the air with sharpness as she hurled accusations at the doctor.

"Doctor, your treatments have only made our daughter's condition worse!" Mrs. Rodriguez exclaimed, her words dripping with venom. "We trusted you, and now look what's happened!" Dr. Mitchell felt a pang of guilt and unease at the harshness of Mrs. Rodriguez's words, but she knew she had to remain composed in the face of the family's anger.

"I understand you're upset, Mrs. Rodriguez," Dr. Mitchell replied calmly, her voice unwavering despite the onslaught of aggression. "Please know that I've always had your daughter's best interests at heart. Let's work together to find a solution."

But Mrs. Rodriguez was relentless in her attack, her anger boiling over as she continued to berate the doctor for her perceived failures.

"You've done nothing but make empty promises and cause more harm!" Mrs. Rodriguez shouted, her face flushed with anger. "We trusted you, and you've let us down!"

Dr. Mitchell felt the weight of Mrs. Rodriguez's words like a heavy blow, but she knew she had to stay focused on finding a resolution.

"I understand your frustration, Mrs. Rodriguez," Dr. Mitchell responded, her voice tinged with empathy. "I'm committed to reassessing your daughter's treatment plan and exploring alternative options. Let's work together to find a way forward."

Despite Dr. Mitchell's attempts to calm the situation, Mrs. Rodriguez's anger continued to simmer, her accusations ringing in the air like a thunderstorm.

"We don't need your empty promises," Mrs. Rodriguez spat, her voice dripping with contempt. "We need results, and so far, you've given us nothing but disappointment!"

Dr. Mitchell felt a pang of sadness at Mrs. Rodriguez's words, but she remained steadfast in her commitment to finding a solution for their daughter's sake.

"I hear your concerns, Mrs. Rodriguez," Dr. Mitchell replied, her voice steady despite the turmoil around her. "I won't stop until we find a way to improve your daughter's condition. Let's focus on what we can do moving forward."

As Mrs. Rodriguez stormed out of the room, her anger still smoldering, Dr. Mitchell couldn't help but feel the weight of their disappointment. But she remained determined to prove herself worthy of their trust, ready to do whatever it took to help their daughter find relief from her suffering.

Let's break down the strategies employed by Dr. Mitchell in each step of the conversation:

1. Avoiding Obvious Traps:

- Silence or Violence: Despite Mrs. Rodriguez's aggressive behavior, Dr. Mitchell maintained her composure and did not respond with further aggression or defensiveness.
- Making Assumptions: Dr. Mitchell avoided assuming Mrs. Rodriguez's intentions or feelings, instead acknowledging her frustration and addressing her concerns directly.
- Avoiding the Issue: Rather than deflecting or dismissing Mrs. Rodriguez's accusations, Dr. Mitchell acknowledged the seriousness of the situation and committed to finding a solution. - Righteousness: Dr. Mitchell did not assert her authority or righteousness as a doctor but instead empathized with Mrs. Rodriguez's distress and demonstrated a willingness to work together.
- The Blame Game: Dr. Mitchell refrained from blaming Mrs. Rodriguez for her anger or frustration, instead focusing on finding common ground and working collaboratively towards a resolution.

2. Choosing the Best Strategy:

- Ask for Others' Paths: Dr. Mitchell actively listened to Mrs. Rodriguez's concerns, seeking to understand her perspective and emotions despite the aggressive tone.

- Make It Safe: Despite Mrs. Rodriguez's hostility, Dr. Mitchell created a safe space for dialogue by remaining calm, empathetic, and open to discussion.

-       Master My Stories: Dr. Mitchell recognized the emotional impact of Mrs. Rodriguez's accusations and responded with empathy and compassion, acknowledging the gravity of the situation.

-       STATE My Path: Dr. Mitchell confidently shared her commitment to reassessing the treatment plan and exploring alternative options, providing reassurance and a sense of direction in a tumultuous situation. Overall, Dr. Mitchell's approach was characterized by empathy, active listening, and a commitment to addressing Mrs. Rodriguez's concerns with compassion and understanding, despite the aggressive and abusive behavior. By avoiding common communication traps and choosing effective strategies, she aimed to diffuse tension, foster trust, and ultimately work towards a resolution that would benefit their daughter's well-being.

13.Inappropriate billing is being done

In a bustling hospital corridor, Dr. Rodriguez found herself face-to-face with Mr. and Mrs. Johnson, their expressions twisted with anger and frustration. Mrs. Johnson's voice rang out with accusation as she launched into her grievance. "Doctor, we've had enough of these exorbitant bills for treatments we didn't even ask for!" Mrs. Johnson exclaimed, her words sharp with

indignation. "You're taking advantage of our situation, and we won't stand for it any longer!" Dr. Rodriguez felt a pang of discomfort at the harshness of Mrs. Johnson's accusations, but she knew she had to address their concerns with empathy and understanding.

"I hear your frustration, Mrs. Johnson," Dr. Rodriguez replied calmly, her voice steady despite the intensity of the situation. "Please know that our billing practices are transparent, and I'm here to address any discrepancies you may have encountered."

But Mrs. Johnson was relentless in her anger, her voice rising with each word as she continued to berate the doctor for what she perceived as exploitation.

"We're not fooled by your empty reassurances, Doctor!" Mrs. Johnson spat, her eyes blazing with fury. "You're preying on vulnerable patients like us, and it's despicable!"

Dr. Rodriguez took a deep breath, her mind racing with the gravity of the situation. She knew she had to address Mrs. Johnson's concerns with honesty and integrity, despite the hostility of the exchange.

"I understand how concerning this must be for you, Mrs. Johnson," Dr. Rodriguez responded, her voice tinged with empathy. "I assure you that our billing practices adhere to the highest standards of transparency and ethics. Let's review your invoices together and address any discrepancies."

Despite Dr. Rodriguez's attempts to defuse the situation, Mrs. Johnson's anger continued to simmer, her accusations lingering in the air like a bitter cloud.

"We won't be placated by your empty promises, Doctor!" Mrs. Johnson declared, her voice laced with skepticism. "We demand accountability and transparency in our medical care, and we won't rest until we get it!"

Dr. Rodriguez felt a sense of unease at the intensity of Mrs. Johnson's anger, but she remained steadfast in her commitment to addressing their concerns with integrity and honesty. "I hear your demands, Mrs. Johnson," Dr. Rodriguez replied, her voice firm with resolve. "I'm committed to addressing any billing discrepancies and ensuring that you receive the quality care you deserve. Let's work together to find a solution." As Mrs. Johnson stormed out of the room, her anger still palpable, Dr. Rodriguez couldn't help but feel the weight of their distrust. But she remained determined to regain their trust through transparency, accountability, and a renewed commitment to their well-being.

Let's analyze the strategies Dr. Rodriguez utilized in each step of the story:

1.Avoiding Obvious Traps :Silence or Violence: Despite Mrs. Johnson's aggressive demeanor, Dr. Rodriguez remained composed and did not respond with aggression or defensiveness.

-

Making Assumptions
: Dr. Rodriguez avoided assuming Mrs. Johnson's intentions or feelings, instead acknowledging her frustration and addressing her concerns directly. Righteousness: Dr. Rodriguez refrained from asserting her authority or righteousness as a doctor but instead empathized with Mrs. Johnson's distress and demonstrated a willingness to work together towards a resolution.

-The Blame Game: Dr. Rodriguez did not blame Mrs. Johnson for her anger or frustration but instead focused on finding common ground and working collaboratively towards a solution. 2.Choosing the Best Strategy
Ask for Others' Paths
: Dr. Rodriguez actively listened to Mrs. Johnson's concerns, seeking to understand her perspective and emotions despite the aggressive tone.
Make It Safe
Despite Mrs. Johnson's hostility, Dr. Rodriguez created a safe space for dialogue by remaining calm, empathetic, and open to discussion.

STATE My Path

Dr. Rodriguez confidently shared her commitment to addressing any billing discrepancies and ensuring transparency in their medical care, providing reassurance and a sense of direction in a tumultuous situation. Overall, Dr. Rodriguez's approach was characterized by empathy, active listening, and a commitment to addressing Mrs. Johnson's concerns with compassion and understanding, despite the aggressive and accusatory behavior. By avoiding common communication traps and choosing effective strategies, she aimed to diffuse tension, foster trust, and ultimately work towards a resolution that would benefit their patient's well-being.

14.Behaviour of hospital staffs is rude.

In the bustling corridors of St. Mary's Hospital, Mrs. Thompson stormed towards Dr. Patel's office, her face etched with frustration and anger.
Behind her trailed a cacophony of complaints and grievances from various hospital staff members.
"Dr. Patel, I've had enough of this appalling behavior from your staff!" Mrs. Thompson exclaimed, her voice quivering with indignation. "The nurses are rude, the ward boys are dismissive, and even the security guard treated me like a criminal!
This is unacceptable!"
Dr. Patel listened intently, his brow furrowing with concern as he absorbed Mrs. Thompson's grievances. He knew he had to address her concerns with empathy and urgency.
"I hear your frustration, Mrs. Thompson," Dr. Patel responded calmly, his voice measured despite the intensity of the situation. "Please know that your concerns are important to us, and I'm committed to addressing them promptly." But Mrs. Thompson's anger showed no signs of abating as she continued to recount her encounters with the hospital staff.
"The nurses speak to me as if I'm inconveniencing them, and the ward boys ignore my requests for assistance!" Mrs. Thompson exclaimed, her voice rising with each word. "And don't even get me started on the security guard who refused to let me enter the building without a fuss!" Dr. Patel felt a pang of discomfort at Mrs.

Thompson's distress, knowing that such behavior was unacceptable in a healthcare setting. He resolved to investigate the matter thoroughly and take decisive action.

"I understand how distressing this must be for you, Mrs. Thompson," Dr. Patel replied, his tone empathetic. "Please allow me to look into these incidents personally and ensure that appropriate measures are taken to address the behavior of our staff."

Despite Dr. Patel's assurances, Mrs. Thompson's anger persisted, her frustration evident in every word she spoke.

"I won't be satisfied with empty promises, Dr. Patel!" Mrs. Thompson declared, her voice tinged with skepticism. "I demand accountability and respect from your staff, and I won't rest until I receive it!"

Dr. Patel nodded solemnly, his commitment unwavering despite the intensity of Mrs. Thompson's anger.

"I hear your demands, Mrs. Thompson," Dr. Patel responded firmly. "I assure you that I will conduct a thorough investigation into these incidents and take appropriate action to address the behavior of our staff. Your satisfaction and well-being are our top priorities."

As Mrs. Thompson stormed out of his office, her anger still palpable, Dr. Patel couldn't help but feel a sense of urgency. He knew that addressing the behavior of his staff was essential not only for Mrs. Thompson's satisfaction but for the reputation and integrity of St. Mary's Hospital as a whole.

Let's break down the steps and strategies used by Dr. Patel in handling Mrs. Thompson's complaint about the rude behavior of hospital staff:

1.Avoiding Obvious Traps

Silence or Violence

Dr. Patel did not respond with silence or aggression but instead actively listened to Mrs. Thompson's complaints, acknowledging her concerns.

Making Assumptions

Dr. Patel avoided assuming Mrs. Thompson's intentions or feelings, instead focusing on understanding her perspective and addressing her grievances directly.

Righteousness

Despite being in a position of authority as a hospital administrator, Dr. Patel did not assert his authority or righteousness but instead empathized with Mrs. Thompson's distress and demonstrated a commitment to addressing her concerns.

The Blame Game

Dr. Patel did not blame Mrs. Thompson for her frustrations or dismiss her complaints but instead acknowledged the validity of her concerns and expressed a willingness to address them.

2.Choosing the Best Strategy

Ask for Others' Paths

Dr. Patel actively listened to Mrs. Thompson's grievances, seeking to understand her perspective and emotions, despite the intensity of her anger.
Make It Safe
Despite Mrs. Thompson's hostility, Dr. Patel created a safe space for dialogue by remaining calm, empathetic, and open to discussion, reassuring her that her concerns were being taken seriously.

-

STATE My Path
Dr. Patel confidently shared his commitment to investigating the incidents personally and ensuring that appropriate measures were taken to address the behavior of the hospital staff, providing reassurance and a sense of direction in a tumultuous situation. Overall, Dr. Patel's approach was characterized by empathy, active listening, and a commitment to addressing Mrs. Thompson's concerns with compassion and understanding, despite the aggressive and accusatory nature of her complaints. By avoiding common communication traps and choosing effective strategies, he aimed to diffuse tension, foster trust, and ultimately work towards a resolution that would benefit Mrs. Thompson and improve the hospital's overall environment.

15.Patient is Dead bur forcefully kept on ventilator and life support.

In the solemn confines of St. Mark's Hospital, Mr. Johnson paced anxiously outside the intensive care unit (ICU), his heart heavy with grief and frustration. Inside, his beloved wife lay motionless on a hospital bed, connected to a maze of tubes and machines, her fragile form barely recognizable amidst the sterile surroundings.

"Doctor, why is my wife still on life support when there's no hope left?" Mr. Johnson implored, his voice trembling with emotion. "She's gone, but you're keeping her artificially alive against her wishes and mine. This is torture!"

Dr. Ramirez, the attending physician, met Mr. Johnson's anguished gaze with empathy, understanding the weight of his words and the gravity of the situation.

"I understand your pain, Mr. Johnson," Dr. Ramirez replied softly, his tone gentle yet resolute. "Please know that every decision we make here is guided by compassion and a commitment to providing the best possible care for your wlfe."

But Mr. Johnson's anguish only deepened as he recounted the agony of watching his wife's life slip away, trapped in a limbo between life and death.

"You don't understand, Doctor," Mr. Johnson pleaded, tears welling in his eyes. "My wife wouldn't want to be kept alive like this. She deserves dignity and peace, not this endless suffering."

Dr. Ramirez felt a pang of sorrow at Mr. Johnson's anguish, knowing that the decision to withdraw life support was never easy, but he also understood the importance of respecting the wishes of the patient and their loved ones.

"I hear your concerns, Mr. Johnson," Dr. Ramirez responded gently, his voice filled with empathy. "Please trust that we are doing everything we can to provide your wife with the comfort and care she deserves. But I also understand the importance of honoring her wishes and yours." As Mr. Johnson's sobs echoed through the sterile halls of the ICU, Dr. Ramirez knew that he had to tread carefully, balancing compassion with medical ethics and the realities of end-of-life care. "I promise to discuss your concerns with the rest of the medical team and explore all available options," Dr. Ramirez reassured Mr. Johnson, his voice a beacon of hope in the darkness of grief. "Your wife's comfort and well-being are our top priorities, and we will do everything in our power to honor her wishes and provide her with a peaceful transition."

As Dr. Ramirez and Mr. Johnson embraced in a moment of shared sorrow, the weight of their collective grief hung heavy in the air. But amidst the darkness, there was also a glimmer of hope—a shared commitment to ensuring that even in death, dignity and compassion would prevail.

Let's break down the steps and strategies employed by Dr. Ramirez:

1. Avoiding Obvious Traps:

- Silence or Violence: Dr. Ramirez actively engaged with Mr. Johnson's concerns instead of remaining silent or responding aggressively. By acknowledging Mr. Johnson's distress, Dr. Ramirez prevented the conversation from escalating into violence.

- Making Assumptions: Dr. Ramirez avoided assuming Mr. Johnson's intentions or emotions. Instead, he listened attentively to Mr. Johnson's concerns and sought to understand his perspective without judgment.

- Avoiding the Issue: Dr. Ramirez stayed focused on the main issue at hand – Mr. Johnson's distress regarding the continued life support for his deceased wife. He didn't divert the conversation away from this critical topic.

- Righteousness: Instead of asserting his authority or righteousness, Dr. Ramirez acknowledged Mr. Johnson's feelings and concerns with empathy and understanding, fostering an atmosphere of mutual respect and collaboration.

2. Choosing the Best Strategy:

- Ask for Others' Paths: Dr. Ramirez actively listened to Mr. Johnson's concerns, seeking to understand his viewpoint, emotions, and desires regarding his wife's end-of-life care. This approach encouraged open dialogue and demonstrated Dr. Ramirez's willingness to consider Mr. Johnson's perspective.

- 	Make It Safe: Despite the intensity of Mr. Johnson's emotions, Dr. Ramirez created a safe space for discussion by remaining calm, empathetic, and open to dialogue. He reassured Mr. Johnson that his concerns were being heard and respected, fostering trust and mutual understanding. - STATE My Path: Dr. Ramirez confidently shared his commitment to addressing Mr. Johnson's concerns with the medical team and exploring all available options to honor his wife's wishes. By providing reassurance and a clear plan of action, Dr. Ramirez instilled confidence in Mr. Johnson and demonstrated his dedication to resolving the situation with compassion and integrity. In summary, Dr. Ramirez's approach was characterized by empathy, active listening, and a commitment to addressing Mr. Johnson's concerns with compassion and understanding. By avoiding common communication traps and choosing effective strategies, he navigated the conversation successfully, fostering trust and collaboration with Mr. Johnson and working towards a resolution that honored his wife's wishes with dignity and respect.

16. No one is listening when we are calling for a nurse.

In the bustling halls of St. Mary's Hospital, tensions ran high as the relatives of patients found themselves increasingly frustrated with what they perceived as a lack of responsiveness from the nursing staff. Among them were the Johnson family, whose matriarch, Mrs. Johnson, lay in the hospital bed, her condition deteriorating with each passing day.

As the evening descended and the hospital grew quieter, Mrs. Johnson's daughter, Sarah, repeatedly pressed the call button for a nurse, her voice tinged with desperation. "Why isn't anyone coming? We've been waiting for ages!" she exclaimed, her frustration palpable. Dr. Patel, passing by the room, caught sight of the distressed family and immediately approached them, her expression one of concern. "Is everything alright?" she inquired, her tone gentle yet attentive.

Sarah's agitation spilled over as she vented her frustrations. "No, everything is not alright! We've been trying to get a nurse for hours, but no one seems to be listening. My mother needs help, and we're being ignored!"

Recognizing the gravity of the situation, Dr. Patel nodded empathetically, her brow furrowing with concern. "I understand how frustrating this must be for you. Let me personally ensure that someone attends to your mother's needs right away."

With a sense of urgency, Dr. Patel swiftly made her way to the nursing station, where she relayed the Johnson family's concerns to the charge nurse. "The Johnson family has been waiting for assistance, and it's imperative that we respond promptly to their call," she emphasized, her tone firm yet composed.

Meanwhile, back in Mrs. Johnson's room, Sarah's anxiety continued to mount as the minutes ticked by. Just as she was about to press the call button again, a nurse appeared at the doorway, her expression apologetic. "I'm sorry for the delay. How can I assist you?" she asked, her voice gentle and reassuring.

Relief flooded Sarah's features as she explained her mother's needs to the nurse, who immediately sprang into action, attending to Mrs. Johnson with care and efficiency. As the tension in the room eased, Dr. Patel returned, her presence a source of comfort for the beleaguered family.

"I apologize for the delay, Mrs. Johnson. Please know that your concerns have been addressed, and we're here to ensure that you receive the care you need," Dr. Patel reassured, her words infused with sincerity.

Gratitude washed over Sarah as she met Dr. Patel's gaze, her eyes brimming with emotion. "Thank you for listening and for taking action. It means a lot to us," she expressed, her voice tinged with relief.

As Dr. Patel left the room, her heart heavy with the weight of the evening's events, she reflected on the importance of active listening and prompt responsiveness in delivering patient-centered care. Despite the challenges posed by a busy hospital environment, she was determined to uphold the hospital's commitment to compassion and excellence, one patient and family at a time.

Let's break down the steps utilized in Dr. Patel's approach to addressing the concerns raised by the Johnson family about the perceived lack of responsiveness from the nursing staff:

1. Recognizing the Situation:

   - Dr. Patel noticed the distress of the Johnson family as they repeatedly tried to call for a nurse. She recognized the urgency of the situation and understood the need to intervene promptly.

2. Approaching with Empathy:

   - Dr. Patel approached the family with genuine concern, acknowledging their frustration and distress. Her empathetic approach helped to establish trust and rapport with the family, creating a conducive environment for communication.

3. Active Listening:

   - Dr. Patel actively listened to Sarah's concerns without interrupting, allowing her to express her frustrations fully. This demonstrated Dr. Patel's commitment to understanding the family's perspective and validating their emotions.

4. Assurance and Action:

\-   Dr. Patel assured the family that she would personally ensure that their concerns were addressed promptly. This reassurance provided the family with a sense of validation and confidence that their needs would be met. 5. Effective Communication with Nursing Staff:

\-   Dr. Patel effectively communicated the Johnson family's concerns to the charge nurse, emphasizing the importance of prompt responsiveness to patient needs. Her clear and assertive communication helped to facilitate timely action from the nursing staff.

6. Prompt Resolution:

\-   Dr. Patel's intervention led to prompt action from the nursing staff, with a nurse arriving at the Johnson family's room to assist them shortly after Dr. Patel's communication with the charge nurse. This demonstrated Dr. Patel's commitment to ensuring that patient needs were addressed without delay.

7. Reassurance and Support:

\-   Dr. Patel reassured the Johnson family that their concerns had been heard and addressed, providing them with a sense of comfort and support during a challenging time. Her presence and words of reassurance helped to alleviate the family's anxiety and restore their trust in the healthcare team.

8. Gratitude and Acknowledgment:

\-   The Johnson family expressed gratitude to Dr. Patel for her intervention and support, acknowledging the impact of her actions on their experience. This acknowledgment reinforced the importance of effective communication and advocacy in patient care. Overall, Dr. Patel's approach was characterized by empathy, active listening, effective communication, and prompt action. By addressing the concerns of the Johnson family with compassion and professionalism, she was able to facilitate a positive outcome and uphold the hospital's commitment to patientcentered care.

17.Paper work takes too much time

In a bustling hospital corridor, amidst the flurry of activity, the Patel family found themselves growing increasingly impatient. Their matriarch, Mrs. Patel, lay in her hospital bed, her condition stable but requiring ongoing care. As the afternoon wore on, Mr. Patel glanced anxiously at his watch, his frustration mounting with each passing minute.

"We've been waiting for hours," he muttered to his wife, his tone tinged with impatience. "I can't believe how long this paperwork is taking. We need to leave soon."

Mrs. Patel nodded in agreement, her expression weary. "I know, dear. But they said we can't go until all the paperwork is sorted. It's taking forever."

Just then, Dr. Smith, the attending physician, approached the Patel family, her demeanor calm and composed. "I understand you've been waiting for quite some time. I apologize for the delay," she said, her voice tinged with empathy.

Mr. Patel's frustration bubbled to the surface as he vented his concerns to Dr. Smith. "We appreciate the care here, but this paperwork is taking too long. We have other commitments and need to leave soon."

Dr. Smith listened attentively, nodding in understanding. "I completely understand your situation. Let me see what I can do to expedite the process," she assured them, her tone reassuring.

With a sense of urgency, Dr. Smith made her way to the nursing station, where she spoke with the administrative staff responsible for the paperwork. "The Patel family is growing anxious about the delay in completing their paperwork. Is there anything we can do to streamline the process?" she inquired, her tone professional yet assertive.

Meanwhile, back in Mrs. Patel's room, the family's anxiety continued to mount as they waited for an update. Just as they were beginning to lose hope, a nurse appeared at the doorway, a stack of papers in hand. "I apologize for the delay. Here are the completed forms," she said, her tone apologetic.

Relief washed over the Patel family as they reviewed the paperwork, their gratitude evident. "Thank you for your help. We appreciate you getting this sorted out quickly," Mrs. Patel expressed, her voice filled with relief.

Dr. Smith returned to the Patel family's room, a smile of satisfaction gracing her lips. "I'm pleased to inform you that the paperwork has been completed. You're free to leave whenever you're ready," she announced, her tone warm and inviting.

As the Patel family prepared to depart, Dr. Smith extended her well wishes. "Take care, Mrs. Patel. And don't hesitate to reach out if you need anything further," she said, her genuine concern evident.

With a sense of gratitude for the care they had received, the Patel family bid farewell to the hospital staff, their hearts filled with appreciation for their dedication and professionalism.

Let's break down the steps involved in Dr. Smith's approach to addressing the Patel family's concerns about the lengthy paperwork process:

1. Acknowledging the Concerns:

-        Dr. Smith noticed the growing impatience and frustration of the Patel family regarding the paperwork delay. She recognized the need to address their concerns promptly to ensure a positive patient experience. 2. Approaching with Empathy:

-        Dr. Smith approached the Patel family with empathy, acknowledging their frustration and expressing understanding for their situation. This empathetic approach helped to establish rapport and trust with the family.

3. Active Listening:

   - Dr. Smith actively listened to Mr. Patel's concerns about the prolonged paperwork process, allowing him to voice his frustrations fully without interruption. This demonstrated Dr. Smith's commitment to understanding the family's perspective and validating their emotions.

4. Assurance and Action:

-        Dr. Smith assured the Patel family that she would take action to expedite the paperwork process. This assurance provided the family with a sense of validation and confidence that their concerns were being addressed. 5. Effective Communication with Staff:

-        Dr. Smith effectively communicated the Patel family's concerns to the administrative staff responsible for the paperwork process. Her clear and assertive communication emphasized the importance of addressing the issue promptly.

6. Prompt Resolution:

  - Dr. Smith's intervention led to prompt action from the administrative staff, resulting in the completion of the paperwork in a timely manner. This demonstrated Dr. Smith's commitment to ensuring that patient needs were met efficiently.

7. Reassurance and Support:

  - Dr. Smith reassured the Patel family that the paperwork had been completed and they were free to leave. Her presence and words of reassurance provided the family with a sense of comfort and support during a stressful time.

8. Follow-Up and Closure:

  - Dr. Smith extended her well wishes to the Patel family as they prepared to depart, emphasizing that they could reach out if they needed further assistance. This follow-up ensured that the family felt supported and valued even after their concerns had been addressed. Overall, Dr. Smith's approach was characterized by empathy, active listening, effective communication, and prompt action. By addressing the Patel family's concerns with compassion and professionalism, she was able to facilitate a positive resolution and uphold the hospital's commitment to patient-centered care.

18.Few Relative are inherently ill mouthed and rude.

In this , Dr. Patel encountered Mr. and Mrs. Smith, known for their rude and ill-mouthed behavior, while making her rounds at St. Mary's
Hospital. Their daughter, Emily, was hospitalized in the ICU, adding an extra layer of stress and tension to the situation.

Dr. Patel approached the Smiths with a warm smile, demonstrating her professionalism and willingness to engage with them despite their reputation. She greeted them courteously and inquired about Emily's condition, setting a positive tone for the conversation. However, Mr. Smith's immediate response was confrontational, as he launched into a tirade about the perceived shortcomings of the hospital staff and the lack of progress in Emily's treatment. Dr. Patel recognized the need to address his concerns promptly to prevent the situation from escalating further.

Maintaining her composure, Dr. Patel acknowledged Mr. Smith's concerns and assured him that she would personally check Emily's chart to provide an update on her condition. This response demonstrated her commitment to addressing their worries and providing transparent communication.

As Dr. Patel continued to engage with the Smiths, Mrs. Smith's impatience and frustration became apparent, adding another layer of complexity to the interaction. Despite the challenging circumstances, Dr. Patel remained focused on addressing their concerns and providing reassurance.

She reiterated the hospital's dedication to Emily's care and promised to consult with her attending physician to ensure they received a comprehensive update. This proactive approach helped to defuse some of the tension in the room and provided the Smiths with a sense of confidence in the medical team's efforts. Throughout the interaction, Dr. Patel demonstrated empathy, patience, and professionalism, recognizing that the Smiths' behavior stemmed from fear and anxiety about Emily's condition. By remaining steadfast in her commitment to providing compassionate care, Dr. Patel was able to navigate the encounter successfully, despite the inherent challenges posed by the Smiths' rude and illmouthed behavior.

After providing the Smiths with a detailed update on Emily's condition, Dr. Patel noticed a subtle shift in their demeanor, indicating a potential easing of tensions. She expressed gratitude for their patience and understanding, reinforcing the importance of collaboration and mutual respect in overcoming obstacles during difficult times.

Overall, Dr. Patel's approach exemplified the principles of effective communication and compassionate care, highlighting the importance of empathy, patience, and professionalism in navigating challenging situations with inherently illmouthed and rude individuals.

let's break down the steps and strategies employed by Dr. Patel in dealing with the inherently illmouthed and rude relatives:

1.Recognizing the Situation

Dr. Patel acknowledged the reputation of Mr. and Mrs. Smith for being ill-mouthed and rude. Understanding the potential challenges posed by such individuals, she prepared herself mentally to handle the encounter with patience and professionalism.

2.Approaching with Calmness and Warmth

Dr. Patel greeted Mr. and Mrs. Smith with a warm smile and courteous demeanor. Despite knowing their reputation, she maintained a calm and composed attitude, setting a positive tone for the conversation and demonstrating her willingness to engage constructively.

3.Active Listening

 When Mr. Smith expressed his frustrations and concerns, Dr. Patel actively listened without interrupting. By allowing Mr. Smith to voice his grievances, she demonstrated empathy and respect for his emotions, even in the face of hostility.

4.Empathetic Response

Dr. Patel responded empathetically to Mr. Smith's concerns, acknowledging his frustrations and assuring him that she would address them promptly. This approach helped to validate Mr. Smith's feelings and create a sense of understanding between them. 5.Transparency and Reassurance

Dr. Patel was transparent about her intentions to review Emily's medical records and consult with her attending physician to provide a comprehensive update. This transparency reassured Mr. Smith that his concerns were being taken seriously and addressed promptly, helping to alleviate some of his anxieties.

6.Maintaining Professionalism

- Despite the confrontational demeanor of Mr. and Mrs. Smith, Dr. Patel maintained her professionalism throughout the interaction. She refrained from responding defensively or engaging in argumentative behavior, instead focusing on addressing their concerns with empathy and understanding.

7.Proactive Problem-Solving

Dr. Patel took a proactive approach to problem-solving by offering to consult with Emily's attending physician to ensure the Smiths received the information they needed. This proactive stance demonstrated Dr. Patel's commitment to resolving the situation effectively and fostering collaboration with the family.

8.Expressing Gratitude

At the conclusion of the interaction, Dr. Patel expressed gratitude to Mr. and Mrs. Smith for their patience and understanding. This expression of gratitude helped to reinforce the importance of mutual respect and collaboration in overcoming challenges during difficult times.

Overall, Dr. Patel's approach was characterized by empathy, active listening, transparency, and professionalism. By employing these strategies, she was able to navigate a challenging encounter with inherently ill-mouthed and rude relatives, fostering understanding and cooperation while addressing their concerns with compassion and respect.

19.Change My doctor,I am not satisfied

Addressing the concern about changing doctors involves navigating the delicate balance of respecting the patient's autonomy while ensuring they receive appropriate care. Here's how it could unfold:

Patient's Relative (Mr. Johnson): Dr. Smith, I need to talk to you. We're not satisfied with the care our family member is receiving. We want to change doctors.

Dr. Smith: I understand your concern, Mr. Johnson. Can you please tell me more about what's been troubling you?

Mr. Johnson: Well, to be honest, we feel like our current doctor isn't giving us the attention and care we expect. We want someone who listens to us and is more proactive in managing our family member's health.

Dr. Smith: I'm sorry to hear that you're feeling this way. Your feedback is valuable, and I want to assure you that your family member's well-being is our top priority. Would you mind sharing specific instances where you felt the care was lacking?

Mr. Johnson: Sure. For one, we often feel rushed during appointments, like our concerns aren't being fully addressed. And there have been a couple of times when we felt like important issues were overlooked.

Dr. Smith: I appreciate you sharing your experiences. It's essential for us to address any concerns you have and ensure you feel heard and supported. If you're open to it, I'd like to discuss potential solutions to improve your experience with our current doctor. However, if you still feel strongly about changing doctors, I can assist you with that process as well.

Mr. Johnson: Thank you, Dr. Smith. We appreciate your willingness to listen and help us find the best solution for our family member's care.

Dr. Smith: Of course, Mr. Johnson. I'll arrange a meeting with our patient advocacy team to discuss your concerns further and explore all available options. In the meantime, if there's anything specific you'd like to address or if you have any questions, please don't hesitate to reach out to me.

In this , Dr. Smith demonstrates effective communication by actively listening to the patient's relative, acknowledging their concerns, and offering potential solutions. While advocating for the current doctor, Dr. Smith also respects the patient's right to seek care that aligns with their preferences and needs.

Here's an explanation of the steps taken by Dr. Smith to address the concern about changing doctors:

1. Active Listening and Empathy:
   - Dr. Smith begins by actively listening to Mr. Johnson's concerns about wanting to change doctors. She approaches the conversation with empathy, acknowledging Mr. Johnson's feelings and validating his experience.

2. Clarifying the Concerns:

-        Dr. Smith seeks clarification from Mr. Johnson to understand the specific reasons behind the desire to change doctors. By asking open-ended questions, she encourages Mr. Johnson to express his concerns fully. 3. Validation and Assurance:

-        Dr. Smith validates Mr. Johnson's concerns, expressing understanding for his perspective and assuring him that his feedback is valued. This helps to build trust and rapport with the patient's family.
4. Exploring Solutions:

  - Dr. Smith offers to discuss potential solutions to address the concerns with the current doctor. She emphasizes her commitment to resolving any issues and improving the patient's care experience.
5. Respecting Patient Autonomy:

-        While advocating for the current doctor and suggesting ways to improve the care experience, Dr. Smith respects Mr. Johnson's autonomy and acknowledges his right to seek care that aligns with his preferences and needs. 6. Offering Assistance with the Change Process: -   Dr. Smith acknowledges Mr. Johnson's desire to change doctors and offers her assistance with the process. She assures him that she will facilitate the transition smoothly and ensure continuity of care for the patient.

7. Follow-Up and Support:

- Dr. Smith concludes the conversation by expressing her willingness to help and offering ongoing support. She assures Mr. Johnson that she will arrange further discussions with the patient advocacy team to address his concerns comprehensively.

Overall, Dr. Smith demonstrates effective communication and patient-centered care by actively listening, validating concerns, exploring solutions, and offering support throughout the process of addressing the patient's family's concerns about changing doctors.

20.My patient came walking and was well before.Understanding a Progressive Disease

Setting: Hospital Consultation Room
Characters:
- Dr. Smith: The doctor on duty.
- Mr. and Mrs. Patel: Relatives of the patient.
- Nurse Taylor: Assisting Dr. Smith.
- Patient: Mr. Patel's brother, admitted with fever and mild shortness of breath.

Narrator:
The patient arrived at the hospital with mild symptoms but has progressively worsened despite treatment. His relatives believe the hospital treatment is to blame for his deterioration. Dr. Smith must explain the nature of the patient's progressive disease and the severity of his condition.

Dr. Smith (calmly and empathetically):
"Mr. and Mrs. Patel, thank you for meeting with me. I understand you're concerned about your brother's condition, and I want to address your worries."

Mr. Patel (frustrated):

"Doctor, when he came here, he was just fine. He was walking, eating, and full of energy. Now, he's in the ICU and getting worse every day. What happened?"

Mrs. Patel (tearfully):
"We trusted the hospital to take care of him. How did he end up like this?"

Dr. Smith (sharing facts and telling the story):
"I understand your frustration and worry. When your brother first arrived, he did have mild symptoms, but after further testing, we diagnosed him with a progressive disease that can worsen over time. Initially, it presented with just fever and shortness of breath, but as it progresses, it can severely impact the body's functions."

Mr. Patel (angrily):
"But he was fine before the treatment here. Are you saying the treatment made him worse?"

Dr. Smith (making it safe and talking tentatively):
"I understand how it might seem that way, but the progression we're seeing is due to the nature of his disease, not the treatment. We've been doing everything possible to manage his symptoms and slow the progression, but some diseases can advance rapidly despite our best efforts."

Mrs. Patel (confused):

"So, what exactly is wrong with him? Why didn't we know it was this serious?"

Dr. Smith (mastering his story and providing reassurance):
"Your brother has a condition that can escalate quickly, often starting with mild symptoms before becoming severe. It's not uncommon for such diseases to appear manageable initially, only to worsen rapidly. This is why he seemed fine at first but deteriorated over time."

Mr. Patel (calmer but still concerned):
"Is there nothing more you can do? We just want him to get better."

Dr. Smith (avoiding the fool's choice and providing support):
"We are using all available treatments to support him and manage his symptoms. Sometimes, even with the best care, a disease can progress in ways we can't fully control. Our goal is to give him the best possible care and support."

Mrs. Patel (tearfully):
"We don't want to lose him. Is there any hope?"

Dr. Smith (compassionately and realistically):
"We are monitoring him closely and adjusting treatments as needed. While the disease is serious, we are committed to doing everything we can. It's

important to stay hopeful, but also to understand the gravity of the situation."

Nurse Taylor (offering additional support):
"We're here to support you and answer any questions you have. If you need more information or just someone to talk to, please let us know."

Mr. Patel (appreciatively):
"Thank you, Doctor. We just want to make sure he's getting the best care."

Dr. Smith (reassuringly):
"He is receiving the best care possible. We're all dedicated to his well-being, and we're here to support both him and your family through this challenging time."

Narrator:
Dr. Smith and Nurse Taylor utilized a range of effective communication strategies to address the Patels' concerns and explain the progressive nature of the disease. This helped the relatives understand the severity of the situation and reassured them that everything possible is being done for their loved one.

Analysis of Communication Strategies Utilized

1. Empathy and Compassion:
- What Dr. Smith did: Acknowledged the relatives' concerns and emotional pain. - Purpose: Builds trust and rapport, making it easier for the relatives to process difficult information.

Example:
> "I understand you're concerned about your brother's condition, and I want to address your worries."

2. Sharing Facts and Telling the Story:
- What Dr. Smith did: Explained the progressive nature of the disease and its typical course. - Purpose: Provides clarity and helps the relatives understand why the patient's condition worsened.

Example:
> "When your brother first arrived, he did have mild symptoms, but after further testing, we diagnosed him with a progressive disease that can worsen over time."

3. Making It Safe and Talking Tentatively:
-        What Dr. Smith did: Used gentle language and acknowledged how the situation might appear to the relatives.

-        Purpose: Reduces defensive reactions and makes it easier for the relatives to express their concerns.

Example:

> "I understand how it might seem that way, but the progression we're seeing is due to the nature of his disease, not the treatment."

4. Mastering His Story and Providing Reassurance:

-        What Dr. Smith did: Provided a clear explanation of the disease's progression and reassured the relatives of the care being provided.

-        Purpose: Helps align the relatives' understanding with the medical reality and reassures them about the care being given.

Example:
> "Your brother has a condition that can escalate quickly, often starting with mild symptoms before becoming severe."

5. Avoiding the Fool's Choice and Providing Support:

-        What Dr. Smith did: Reassured the relatives that all possible treatments are being used and offered support without making it seem like there is no hope.

-        Purpose: Balances hope with realism and ensures that the relatives feel supported and informed.

Example:
> "We are using all available treatments to support him and manage his symptoms. Sometimes, even with the best care, a disease can progress in ways we can't fully control."

6. Offering Additional Support:
- What Nurse Taylor did: Reassured the relatives of ongoing support and availability for questions.
- Purpose: Provides a sense of security and ensures the relatives know they are not alone.

Example:
> "We're here to support you and answer any questions you have. If you need more information or just someone to talk to, please let us know."

Summary

Dr. Smith and Nurse Taylor effectively used empathy, clear communication, and supportive dialogue to help the Patels understand the progressive nature of their brother's disease. By sharing facts, making the conversation safe, providing reassurance, avoiding the fool's choice, and offering additional support, they addressed the relatives' concerns and helped them process the gravity of the situation. This approach ensured that the conversation was conducted with sensitivity, respect, and compassion, helping the relatives accept the reality of their loved one's condition.

21. Change in Diagnosis and Specialist

Setting: Hospital Room
Characters:
- Dr. Green: The primary care doctor.
- Mr. and Mrs. Sharma: Relatives of the patient.
- Patient: Mrs. Sharma's father, admitted with initial symptoms that have now progressed.
Narrator:
Mrs. Sharma's father was admitted to the hospital with an initial diagnosis. However, his condition has developed new complications, requiring a transfer to another specialty. Dr. Green must explain the situation and the reasons for the change to the anxious relatives.
Dr. Green (calmly and empathetically):
"Mr. and Mrs. Sharma, thank you for taking the time to meet with me. I understand that this is a very challenging time for you both."   Mr. Sharma (concerned):
"Doctor, we're really worried. He was under your care initially. Why is there a need to change his doctor now?"
 Mrs. Sharma (anxiously):
"Yes, we need to know why this is happening. Is his condition getting worse?"   Dr. Green (sharing facts and telling the story):
"I understand your concerns. Initially, your father was admitted with symptoms that fell under my area of specialty. We provided the appropriate treatment based on that initial diagnosis. However, over the past

few days, his condition has developed new complications that require the expertise of another specialty." Mr. Sharma (worried):

"But why can't you continue to treat him? Why do we need another doctor now?" Dr. Green (making it safe and talking tentatively):

"It's natural to feel worried about a change like this. The complications he's developed are best managed by a specialist who has specific expertise in this new area. This change is to ensure he receives the best possible care tailored to his current needs." Mrs. Sharma (tearfully):

"What kind of complications are we talking about? Is it very serious?" Dr. Green (explaining and setting expectations):

"The complications are indeed serious, but transferring him to another specialty doesn't mean we're giving up. It means we are bringing in the right expert to handle these new issues effectively. The specialist will conduct further evaluations and provide a treatment plan that is more suited to his current condition." Mr. Sharma (anxiously):

"So, what happens now? Will this delay his treatment?" Dr. Green (reassuring and providing clarity):

"There will be no delay. We are coordinating closely with the specialist, and the transition will be smooth. The new specialist will review all the information and start the necessary treatment immediately. Our goal is to ensure he receives the most appropriate and timely care." Mrs. Sharma (calming slightly):

"Will we be able to meet this new doctor? We want to understand what's happening." Dr. Green (building trust and offering support):
"Absolutely. The new specialist will meet with you as soon as possible to discuss the new treatment plan and answer any questions you may have. I will also be available to support you during this transition and ensure you have all the information you need." Mr. Sharma (more composed):
"Thank you, Dr. Green. We just want to make sure he's getting the best care." Dr. Green (compassionately):
"I understand completely. This change is all about providing the best possible care for him. If you have any concerns or need further information at any point, please don't hesitate to reach out to me. We're here to support you and your father through this." Mrs. Sharma (nodding):
"Thank you, Doctor. We appreciate your help and understanding." Dr. Green (smiling reassuringly):
"You're welcome. We'll take good care of him and keep you updated every step of the way. Let's focus on getting him the care he needs right now." Narrator: Through calm, empathetic communication, Dr. Green was able to reassure Mr. and Mrs. Sharma about the need for the change in specialist. By sharing facts, making it safe for them to express their concerns, and providing clear information about what to expect, Dr. Green helped alleviate their anxiety and built trust in the medical team's decision.
Analysis of Communication Strategies Utilized

1. Empathy and Compassion:
- What Dr. Green did: Acknowledged the relatives' stress and emotional pain.
- Purpose: Builds trust and rapport, making it easier for the relatives to process difficult information.
 Example:
> "I understand that this is a very challenging time for you both."
2. Sharing Facts and Telling the Story:
- What Dr. Green did: Explained the current situation and the necessity of changing the specialist based on new complications.
- Purpose: Provides clarity and helps the relatives understand the process.

Example:
> "Initially, your father was admitted with symptoms that fell under my area of specialty. We provided the appropriate treatment based on that initial diagnosis. However, over the past few days, his condition has developed new complications that require the expertise of another specialty."
3. Making It Safe and Talking Tentatively:
- What Dr. Green did: Used gentle language and acknowledged the relatives' need for immediate answers.
- Purpose: Reduces defensive reactions and makes it easier for the relatives to express their concerns.

Example:
> "It's natural to feel worried about a change like this."
4. Setting Expectations and Building Trust:
- What Dr. Green did: Provided a timeline for the transition.

22.When nothing is working.Patient Not Improving and Further Interventions Deemed Futile

Setting: Hospital Room   Characters:
- Dr. Smith: The doctor on duty.
- Mr. and Mrs. Johnson: Relatives of the patient.
- Patient: In a bed nearby, condition not improving.

: Difficult Conversation about Treatment Futility

Narrator:
The patient has been in the hospital for several days, and despite various treatments, their condition is not improving. Dr. Smith needs to explain to the anxious relatives that further interventions are unlikely to provide any benefit.

Dr. Smith (calmly and empathetically):
"Mr. and Mrs. Johnson, I appreciate you taking the time to talk with me. I understand how difficult this situation is for you."

Mr. Johnson (anxious):
"Doctor, we're really worried. He's not getting better. Isn't there anything else you can do?"

Mrs. Johnson (tearfully):

"We can't just give up on him. There has to be something more."

Dr. Smith (sharing facts and telling the story):
"I hear your concerns, and I want to assure you that we have tried all the standard and advanced treatments available. Unfortunately, his body isn't responding as we had hoped. Continuing to escalate treatment might not only be ineffective but could also cause more harm and discomfort."

Mr. Johnson (desperate):
"But there must be something! A new drug, a different procedure, something experimental?"

Dr. Smith (making it safe and talking tentatively):
"I understand your desire to explore every possible option. It's completely natural to want to fight for every chance. However, based on my experience and the patient's current condition, I believe that additional aggressive treatments would not improve his situation and could potentially lead to more suffering."

Mrs. Johnson (sobbing):
"So, what are you saying? There's nothing more we can do?"

Dr. Smith (mastering his story and making it safe):
"What I'm saying is that sometimes, the most compassionate choice is to focus on comfort and quality

of life rather than pursuing treatments that are unlikely to help. We can focus on making sure he's comfortable and not in pain."

Mr. Johnson (angrily):
"So, you're just giving up on him?"

Dr. Smith (avoiding the fool's choice and creating a collaborative environment):
"Not at all. We're not giving up on him. Our focus shifts to a different kind of care—palliative care—that prioritizes his comfort and dignity. This doesn't mean we stop caring for him. It means we care for him in the best way possible given his condition."

Mrs. Johnson (calming down slightly):
"What does that involve?"

Dr. Smith (sharing details and asking for their path):
"It involves managing his pain and other symptoms, providing emotional and spiritual support, and helping you and your family through this difficult time. We'll have a dedicated team to support him and you as well. How do you feel about this approach?"

Analysis of Communication Strategies in the Conversation

Dr. Smith's Approach:

1. Sharing Facts and Telling the Story:
- What Dr. Smith did: Explained the current medical condition and the treatments attempted so far,

providing a clear rationale for why further aggressive treatments are unlikely to help.

- Purpose: This helps the relatives understand the medical reality and sets a factual basis for the conversation.

Example:

"I hear your concerns, and I want to assure you that we have tried all the standard and advanced treatments available. Unfortunately, his body isn't responding as we had hoped. Continuing to escalate treatment might not only be ineffective but could also cause more harm and discomfort."

2. Making It Safe and Talking Tentatively:

- What Dr. Smith did: Acknowledged the relatives' desire to explore every possible option and expressed empathy for their situation.

- Purpose: This strategy reassures the relatives that their feelings and concerns are valid, making them feel respected and heard.

Example:

"I understand your desire to explore every possible option. It's completely natural to want to fight for every chance. However, based on my experience and the patient's current condition, I believe that additional aggressive treatments would not improve his situation and could potentially lead to more suffering."

3. Mastering His Story and Making It Safe:

- What Dr. Smith did: Reframed the situation to focus on compassionate care rather than giving up, which helps the relatives see the new approach as a positive step.

- Purpose: This helps to align the doctor's goals with the relatives' desire for the patient's well-being, reducing resistance to the new approach.
  Example:
  "What I'm saying is that sometimes, the most compassionate choice is to focus on comfort and quality of life rather than pursuing treatments that are unlikely to help. We can focus on making sure he's comfortable and not in pain."

4. Avoiding the Fool's Choice and Creating a Collaborative Environment:

- What Dr. Smith did: Explained that shifting to palliative care does not mean giving up, but rather changing the focus of care to what is best for the patient's current condition.

- Purpose: This avoids presenting the situation as a black-and-white choice between continuing aggressive treatment and giving up, instead offering a nuanced approach. **Example**:
  "Not at all. We're not giving up on him. Our focus shifts to a different kind of care—palliative care—that prioritizes his comfort and dignity. This doesn't mean we stop caring for him. It means we care for him in the best way possible given his condition."

5. Sharing Details and Asking for Their Path:

- What Dr. Smith did: Provided specific information about what palliative care involves and invited the relatives to express their feelings and thoughts about this approach.

- Purpose: This engages the relatives in the decision-making process, making them feel involved and respected.

Example:

"It involves managing his pain and other symptoms, providing emotional and spiritual support, and helping you and your family through this difficult time. We'll have a dedicated team to support him and you as well. How do you feel about this approach?"

Summary

In the conversation, Dr. Smith skillfully applied several key strategies from "Crucial Conversations" to manage a delicate and emotionally charged situation. By sharing facts, telling the story, making it safe, talking tentatively, mastering his story, avoiding the fool's choice, and creating a collaborative environment, Dr. Smith was able to guide the relatives towards accepting a palliative care approach. This not only helped in making a difficult situation more manageable but also ensured that the relatives felt heard, respected, and involved in the care of their loved one

23. Breaking the Bad News – Patient is very critical

Scene: Doctor Counsels Aggressive Relatives about a Patient's Critical Condition

Setting: A consultation room in a hospital. Dr. Nayana Deb sits on one side of the table, calm and composed. Across from her are Mr. Sharma and Mrs. Sharma, the patient's son and daughter-in-law, visibly distressed and angry.

Dr. Nayana Deb: (Starting with Heart, speaking gently)
"Mr. and Mrs. Sharma, thank you for coming. I want you to know that we are deeply concerned about Mr. Sharma's condition and are doing everything in our power to support his recovery."

Mr. Sharma: (Raising his voice)
"How can you say that? He was fine yesterday, and now you're saying he's critical? What went wrong?"

Dr. Nayana Deb: (Learning to Look, observing his clenched fists and Mrs. Sharma's tearful eyes)
"I understand how shocking this must feel, Mr. Sharma. It's clear how much you care for your father, and that's why I want to explain everything as clearly as I can."
(Pauses to allow space for their emotions)

Mrs. Sharma: (Angrily)
"Explain? Isn't it too late for explanations? This is negligence!"

Dr. Nayana Deb: (Making It Safe, maintaining a calm tone)

"I hear your frustration, Mrs. Sharma. Let's take a moment to discuss what's happening in detail. My goal is to ensure you feel informed and involved in every decision regarding his care."

Mr. Sharma: (Still agitated)
"Then tell us—what exactly is wrong with him now?"

Dr. Nayana Deb: (Mastering My Stories, focusing on facts)
"Over the last 24 hours, Mr. Sharma's condition worsened due to complications. His organs are under significant stress, and he is struggling with severe metabolic and respiratory imbalances. Despite all interventions, his condition remains very critical."

Mrs. Sharma: (Sobbing)
"You should have done more earlier! Why didn't you do something sooner?"

Dr. Nayana Deb: (State My Path, calmly explaining)
"I understand your concern, Mrs. Sharma. Over the past few days, we've been addressing his complications step by step. Unfortunately, his body's response has been weaker than we hoped. I want to assure you that our team has been vigilant and proactive throughout."

Mr. Sharma: (Leaning forward aggressively)
"So, what's the plan now? Or are you just going to give up?"

Dr. Nayana Deb: (Exploring Others' Paths, acknowledging their feelings)
"I can see how worried and angry you are, Mr. Sharma,

and those feelings are valid. This is a very difficult time, and you want to know that everything possible is being done for your father. Let me explain our current plan and hear your thoughts."

"Right now, we are focusing on stabilizing his condition through intensive monitoring, medication, and supportive therapies. However, the risks remain high, and I want to prepare you for all possibilities."

Mrs. Sharma: (Softer now, through tears)
"What do you mean by all possibilities?"

Dr. Nayana Deb: (Compassionately)
"It means we are doing everything we can to help him recover, but there is a chance his body might not respond to the treatment. I want us to be prepared for any outcome, while continuing to give him the best care possible."

Mr. Sharma: (Taking a deep breath, calming slightly)
"So what can we do now?"

Dr. Nayana Deb: (Moving to Action, collaboratively deciding next steps)
"The most important thing right now is to let the team focus on his immediate care. At the same time, if there are any rituals or specific things you'd like to do for him, we can accommodate them. I'll also ensure you're updated frequently about any changes."

Mrs. Sharma: (Nodding)
"Okay... but promise us you won't give up on him."

Dr. Nayana Deb: (Reassuring)
"I promise you, our team is dedicated to doing everything we can for him. If there's anything you'd like to discuss further or ask, please let me know."

Mr. Sharma: (Sighing, visibly calmer)
"Thank you for explaining, Doctor. We just want him to be okay."

Dr. Nayana Deb: (With empathy)
"I understand, and I'll do everything in my power to support him and your family during this time."

Narration:
This dialogue demonstrates the balance of addressing the relatives' aggressive reactions with calmness and clarity. By providing a safe space for their emotions, validating their concerns, and collaboratively planning next steps, the doctor helps diffuse tension and maintain productive communication

Scene: Doctor Counsels Aggressive Relatives about a Patient's Death

Setting: A private consultation room in the hospital. Dr. Nayana Deb sits on one side of the table, her demeanor calm and empathetic. Across from her are Mr. Sharma and Mrs. Sharma, the patient's son and daughter-in-law, visibly agitated and anxious.

Dr. Nayana Deb: (Starting with Heart, speaking gently)
"Mr. and Mrs. Sharma, thank you for taking the time to meet with me. I want to start by saying how deeply sorry I am about what I need to share with you today. We've been doing everything we could to support Mr. Sharma's recovery."

Mr. Sharma: (Raising his voice, tense)
"What do you mean? How is he now? Why are you talking like this?"

Dr. Nayana Deb: (Learning to Look, noticing his clenched fists and Mrs. Sharma's teary eyes)
"I can see how worried and upset you are, and I want to explain everything clearly. I am deeply sorry to inform you that Mr. Sharma passed away earlier this morning."
(Pauses to allow the information to sink in)

Mrs. Sharma: (Breaking down)
"No... no, this can't be true! He was alive yesterday! How did this happen?"

Mr. Sharma: (Slamming his hand on the table, angry)
"What did you do? Why couldn't you save him? This is unacceptable!"

Dr. Nayana Deb: (Making It Safe, speaking calmly)
"Mr. Sharma, I can see how much you're hurting, and I completely understand your anger and frustration. You cared so deeply for him, and this loss is devastating. Let me explain everything step by step so you have a clear picture of what happened."

Mr. Sharma: (Still agitated)
"Go on then, explain!"

Dr. Nayana Deb: (Mastering My Stories, sticking to the facts)
"Over the past few days, Mr. Sharma's condition worsened due to multiple complications, including severe metabolic and respiratory distress. Despite our intensive interventions—medications, supportive therapies, and constant monitoring—his body could no longer sustain itself. Early this morning, his heart stopped, and despite all resuscitation efforts, we were unable to bring him back."

Mrs. Sharma: (Crying)
"Was he in pain? Did he suffer?"

Dr. Nayana Deb: (Compassionately)
"No, he wasn't in pain. We ensured he was kept comfortable and peaceful in his final moments. He passed away with dignity, surrounded by care."

Mr. Sharma: (Voice trembling)
"Why didn't you tell us sooner? We should have been there!"

Dr. Nayana Deb: (Acknowledging their feelings)
"I understand how important it was for you to be with him. Everything happened so quickly, and our priority was to focus on his care in those critical moments. I deeply regret that you couldn't be there."

Mrs. Sharma: (Sobbing)
"What do we do now? How do we even process this?"

Dr. Nayana Deb: (Moving to Action, offering support)
"Take all the time you need right now. When you feel ready, I'll guide you through the next steps, whether it's viewing him, making arrangements, or talking to someone from our support team. Please know that I'm here for you, and you're not alone in this."

Mr. Sharma: (Calming slightly, sighing deeply)
"We just wanted him to come back home... this is so hard."

Dr. Nayana Deb: (Empathetically)
"I know this is an incredibly painful time for your family. If there's anything you need—whether it's questions, support, or just someone to talk to—please don't hesitate to reach out. We'll do everything we can to support you through this."

Mrs. Sharma: (Nodding through tears)
"Thank you, Doctor... for everything."

Narration:
This dialogue showcases how to break the news of a patient's death with compassion and clarity while addressing the relatives' anger and grief. By creating a safe environment, providing clear explanations, and offering ongoing support, the doctor helps the family process their emotions and begin navigating the next steps.

24.Patient is still alive but you are declairing him dead

.

Setting: Emergency Department, Hospital **Characters:**

- **Dr. Smith**: The doctor on duty.
- **Mrs. Anderson**: The mother of the teenager.
- **Nurse Taylor**: Assisting Dr. Smith.
- **John**: The teenager, on a ventilator, unresponsive.

Narrator: John, a teenager, has been brought to the emergency department after a severe accident. Despite the medical team's best efforts, John has succumbed to his injuries. Dr. Smith now faces the painful task of explaining the situation to his mother, Mrs. Anderson, who is in deep denial.

Dr. Smith (gently): "Mrs. Anderson, can we talk for a moment?"

Mrs. Anderson (tearfully but hopeful): "Doctor, please. He's still breathing. Look, his chest is moving. He's still warm. He's not gone. He can't be."

Dr. Smith (empathetically, placing a hand on her shoulder): "I understand this is incredibly difficult, and I wish the news were different. The movement you're seeing is from the ventilator, which is mechanically moving his chest. It's not a sign of life, but a function of the machine." **Mrs. Anderson (frantically):** "No, no, he's just in a deep sleep. I know he'll wake up. He's my boy; he's a fighter."

Dr. Smith (calmly): "I know how much you want to believe that, and it's perfectly normal to feel this way. But John's injuries were too severe for him to recover. We've done everything we can, but his heart has stopped, and his brain is no longer functioning."

Mrs. Anderson (desperate): "But he's still warm. If he's dead, how can he be warm?" **Dr. Smith (softly):** "The warmth you feel is because his body hasn't yet cooled down. This is a natural process that happens after death. It doesn't mean that he's still alive."

Nurse Taylor (supportively): "We're here to help you through this, Mrs. Anderson. It's okay to ask questions and express your feelings."

Mrs. Anderson (clinging to hope): "There must be something more you can do. Another doctor, another treatment. Please, don't give up on him."

Dr. Smith (firm but compassionate): "We've consulted with all the specialists and used every available treatment. I wish there was more we could do, but John's body has reached a point where it can no longer sustain life."

Mrs. Anderson (angrily): "How can you be so sure? What if you're wrong?"

Dr. Smith (gently): "I wish I could offer you different news. The tests we've conducted show no brain activity, and his heart has stopped despite our efforts. These are definitive signs that he has passed away."

Mrs. Anderson (sobbing uncontrollably): "No, no, this can't be true. He was just here, full of life. How can he be gone?"

Dr. Smith (supportive): "I know this is so hard to accept. Losing a child is the most painful experience a parent can endure. We're here to support you in any way we can."

Nurse Taylor (handing tissues to Mrs. Anderson): "Would you like to hold his hand or spend some time with him? We want to give you as much time as you need."

Mrs. Anderson (crying but calmer): "I just want to be with him. I don't know how to say goodbye."

Dr. Smith (softly): "Take all the time you need, Mrs. Anderson. We're here for you, and we'll help you through every step."

Mrs. Anderson (holding John's hand, tears streaming down her face): "Thank you, Doctor. I just can't believe this is happening."

Dr. Smith (compassionately): "I'm so sorry for your loss. If you have any questions or need anything, please let us know. We'll be right here."

Narrator: Through compassionate and clear communication, Dr. Smith helps Mrs. Anderson face the heartbreaking reality of her son's death. The support from Nurse Taylor and the respectful approach to Mrs. Anderson's grief provide a space for her to begin processing the loss while feeling cared for by the medical team.

Analysis of Communication Strategies Utilized

1. Empathy and Compassion:
- What Dr. Smith did: From the beginning, Dr. Smith shows empathy by acknowledging Mrs. Anderson's pain and confusion.
- Purpose: Demonstrating empathy helps build a connection and trust, making it easier for Mrs. Anderson to process the difficult information.

Example:
> "I understand this is incredibly difficult, and I wish the news were different."

2. Sharing Facts and Telling the Story:
- What Dr. Smith did: Clearly explained the medical situation, including why the chest movements are not a sign of life and the significance of body warmth post-mortem. - Purpose: Providing clear, factual information helps counter denial and misunderstandings, ensuring that the reality of the situation is communicated effectively.

Example:
> "The movement you're seeing is from the ventilator, which is mechanically moving his chest. It's not a sign of life, but a function of the machine."

3. Making It Safe and Talking Tentatively:
- What Dr. Smith did: Used gentle language and acknowledged Mrs. Anderson's feelings to make her feel heard and respected.

- Purpose: This strategy helps in reducing defensive
reactions and makes it safer for Mrs.
Anderson to express her emotions and thoughts.

Example:
> "I know how much you want to believe that, and it's
perfectly normal to feel this way."

4. Mastering His Story and Making It Safe:
-       What Dr. Smith did: Explained the irreversible
nature of John's condition while maintaining a
compassionate tone.
-       Purpose: Helps in making the harsh reality more
understandable and acceptable by framing it in a
compassionate context.

Example:
> "We've done everything we can, but his heart has
stopped, and his brain is no longer functioning."

5. Providing Reassurance and Support:
-       What Dr. Smith and Nurse Taylor did: Reassured
Mrs. Anderson that they are there to support her and
encouraged her to take her time.
-       Purpose: Offering support and reassuring her
that she is not alone helps in managing the emotional
impact and provides a sense of security during a
traumatic time.

Examples:
> Nurse Taylor: "We're here to help you through this, Mrs. Anderson. It's okay to ask questions and express your feelings."
> Dr. Smith: "Take all the time you need, Mrs. Anderson. We're here for you, and we'll help you through every step."

6. Avoiding the Fool's Choice:
-        What Dr. Smith did: Addressed Mrs. Anderson's plea for further treatments by explaining the finality of the situation without dismissing her emotions.
-        Purpose: This avoids creating a false dichotomy between continuing treatment and giving up, instead framing the situation in a way that acknowledges the complexity and emotional difficulty.

Example:
> "I wish I could offer you different news. The tests we've conducted show no brain activity, and his heart has stopped despite our efforts. These are definitive signs that he has passed away."

7. Asking for Their Path and Collaborative Communication:
-        What Nurse Taylor did: Offered Mrs. Anderson the opportunity to spend time with her son and to express her needs.

-        Purpose: Engaging the family in the process and respecting their need for closure helps in easing the transition and provides them with some control over the situation.

Example:
> "Would you like to hold his hand or spend some time with him? We want to give you as much time as you need."

Summary

Dr. Smith and Nurse Taylor utilized a range of effective communication strategies, including empathy, sharing factual information, making the environment safe for expression, mastering the narrative, providing reassurance, avoiding false choices, and engaging in collaborative communication. These strategies helped to manage Mrs. Anderson's denial and grief, gradually guiding her towards accepting the tragic reality with support and compassion. This approach ensured that the difficult conversation was handled with sensitivity and respect, minimizing additional trauma for Mrs. Anderson.

25.Explaining for organ donation - A Difficult Decision

Setting: Hospital Family Consultation Room

Characters:
- Dr. Smith: The doctor on duty.
- Mrs. and Mr. Johnson: Parents of the patient.
- Nurse Taylor: Assisting Dr. Smith.
- Patient: Their teenage son, now brain dead, in the Intensive Care Unit.

Narrator:
After a severe accident, despite the medical team's best efforts, the teenage boy has been declared brain dead. Dr. Smith must now break the heartbreaking news to the parents and discuss the possibility of organ donation.

Dr. Smith (gently and with empathy):
"Mr. and Mrs. Johnson, I'm so sorry to have to share this news. Your son has sustained severe injuries, and despite all our efforts, he has been declared brain dead. This means that his brain is no longer functioning, and he will not be able to recover."

Mrs. Johnson (in shock, tearfully):

"No, there must be some mistake. He was just here, talking to us. How can this be?"

Mr. Johnson (angrily):
"How can you say that? He looks like he's just sleeping. There must be something more you can do."

Dr. Smith (empathetically and sharing facts):
"I understand this is incredibly difficult to accept. The machines are keeping his heart and lungs working, which is why he appears to be alive. However, the tests we have conducted show no brain activity, and this is an irreversible condition. I wish there were more we could do."

Mrs. Johnson (sobbing):
"So, what happens now? What can we do?"

Dr. Smith (making it safe and talking tentatively):
"This is a devastating moment, and it's hard to find the right words. One way to find some solace in this tragedy is by considering organ donation. This can give other families a chance at life and create a legacy of life through your son."

Mr. Johnson (confused and defensive):
"Organ donation? Are you asking us to let him go and give his organs away?"

Dr. Smith (mastering his story and making it safe):

"I know this is a lot to take in, and the idea of organ donation can be overwhelming at such a difficult time. What I can tell you is that organ donation is a way to honor your son's life by helping others in desperate need. It's entirely your decision, and we will respect whatever you choose."

Nurse Taylor (supportively):
"We're here to support you through every step. If you have any questions about the process or need more time, please let us know. There's no rush in making this decision."

Mrs. Johnson (tearfully but contemplative):
"I just... I don't know. He was so full of life. How can we make this decision now?"

Dr. Smith (providing reassurance and support):
"It's natural to feel uncertain. Many families find that knowing their loved one has saved lives brings a sense of peace and purpose. If you need to talk to other families who have been through this, we can arrange that. It's important that you feel supported and informed in whatever decision you make."

Mr. Johnson (softening, looking at his wife):
"I want to do what's right for him. He always wanted to help people. Maybe this is a way to honor his wishes."

Mrs. Johnson (nodding slowly):

"He was always so generous. If this can help others, maybe it's the right thing to do."

Dr. Smith (supportive and respectful):
"Take your time to think it over. We can answer any questions you have about how the process works and what it involves. Your son's legacy could be the gift of life to others, but it's important you're comfortable with your decision."

Mrs. Johnson (calmer):
"Thank you, Doctor. We'll need a little time to talk it over, but we'll consider it."

Dr. Smith (compassionately):
"Of course. We're here for you, whatever you decide. Take all the time you need, and let us know how we can support you."

Nurse Taylor (offering support):
"If you'd like, I can stay with you to answer any immediate questions or just to be here for support."

Mrs. Johnson (gratefully):
"Thank you. We appreciate your kindness."

Mr. Johnson (with a heavy heart):
"We'll let you know soon. This is a lot to take in."

Dr. Smith (reassuringly):

"We understand. Please know that you're not alone. We're here to help you through this."

Narrator:
Dr. Smith and Nurse Taylor used compassionate and effective communication strategies to support the Johnsons through an incredibly painful decision. By sharing facts, showing empathy, making the environment safe for discussion, and offering support, they helped the parents consider the possibility of organ donation as a way to honor their son's life while respecting their need for time and understanding.

Analysis of Communication Strategies Utilized

1. Empathy and Compassion:
- What Dr. Smith did: Expressed sorrow and understanding for the parents' pain.
- Purpose: Helps build a connection and trust, making it easier for the parents to process the difficult information.

Example:
> "I'm so sorry to have to share this news."

2. Sharing Facts and Telling the Story:
- What Dr. Smith did: Clearly explained the medical condition and the meaning of brain death.

- Purpose: Provides clarity and helps counter denial and misunderstandings.

Example:
> "The machines are keeping his heart and lungs working, which is why he appears to be alive. However, the tests we have conducted show no brain activity, and this is an irreversible condition."

3. Making It Safe and Talking Tentatively:
- What Dr. Smith did: Used gentle language and acknowledged the parents' feelings. - Purpose: Reduces defensive reactions and makes it safer for the parents to express their emotions and thoughts.

Example:
> "This is a devastating moment, and it's hard to find the right words."

4. Mastering His Story and Making It Safe:
- What Dr. Smith did: Reframed the situation to show how organ donation could be a way to honor their son's life.
- Purpose: Helps align the doctor's goals with the parents' desire for their son's legacy.

Example:
> "What I can tell you is that organ donation is a way to honor your son's life by helping others in desperate need."

5. Providing Reassurance and Support:
- What Dr. Smith and Nurse Taylor did: Reassured the
  parents that they have time to make their decision and
  that support is available.
- Purpose: Offers a sense of security and reduces the
  pressure on the parents.

Examples:
> Nurse Taylor: "We're here to support you through
every step. If you have any questions about the process
or need more time, please let us know."
> Dr. Smith: "Take your time to think it over. We can
answer any questions you have about how the process
works and what it involves."

6. Asking for Their Path and Collaborative
Communication:
- What Dr. Smith and Nurse Taylor did: Invited the
  parents to express their thoughts and offered to
  support them regardless of their decision.
- Purpose: Engages the parents in the process and
  respects their need for time and information.

Examples:
> Dr. Smith: "Take your time to think it over. We can
answer any questions you have about how the process
works and what it involves. Your son's legacy could be

the gift of life to others, but it's important you're comfortable with your decision."
> Nurse Taylor: "If you'd like, I can stay with you to answer any immediate questions or just to be here for support."

Summary

In this , Dr. Smith and Nurse Taylor utilized a range of effective communication strategies to handle a delicate and emotional situation. By showing empathy, sharing clear facts, making the conversation safe, reframing the narrative, providing reassurance and support, and engaging in collaborative communication, they helped the Johnsons navigate the painful decision about organ donation. This approach ensured that the conversation was conducted with sensitivity, respect, and compassion, ultimately helping the parents consider organ donation as a way to honor their son's life.

Dr.Pankaj Hans, MD, Consultant Nephrologist.
"Bridging the Gap: Strategies for Connecting with Patients' Families in Healthcare" is an indispensable guide for medical professionals. This book offers practical, real-world strategies to enhance communication, build trust, and effectively manage the emotions of patients' families. By addressing common concerns and providing clear solutions, it empowers doctors to handle even the most challenging situations with confidence and compassion. A must-read for anyone committed to improving patient care and satisfaction.

Dr. Shyam Kishore, MD, DM. Consultant Endocrinology
First Encounter at the Emergency Department
During the initial encounter at the emergency department, it is crucial to create a positive and reassuring impact on the patient's relatives and family members. Your immediate and prompt response, akin to handling a disaster situation, can help keep the relatives calm and reassured.
1. Assessment and Communication:
-Attend to the patient's needs promptly.

- Explain the possible medical ailment to the relatives.

- Discuss treatment modalities, emphasizing thorough evaluation, management, and the plan moving forward.

- Consult with the in-charge consultant for further guidance.
  2. Challenges in Critical Care Services:

- Unfortunately, critical care services are often inadequate in terms of both quantity and quality across many hospitals.

- Healthcare delivery systems vary significantly between countries and even within regions.

- State-run and corporate hospitals offer services of varying quality.

- Given the urgency of the situation, providing optimal medical care to all patients attending the emergency department may not always be feasible.

www.ingramcontent.com/pod-product-compliance
Lightning Source LLC
Chambersburg PA
CBHW061341160726
47995CB00001B/129